D1216401

HERBS AND THE EARTH

• HERBS •
AND THE EARTH

Henry Beston

Woodcuts by John Howard Benson

Dolphin Books
Doubleday & Company, Inc.
Garden City, New York

DOLPHIN BOOKS EDITION 1961, 1973

ISBN: 0-385-03208-0

To two young persons
who never pull up or step on
father's herbs

FOREWORD

Part of the pleasure of writing this book has been the help I have had from others. To my wife, Elizabeth Coatsworth Beston, I would offer thanks for an assistance so constant, so wise and so generously given that without it both manuscript and author would still be missing in the garden. My thanks are due to Mr. Harry E. Maule of Doubleday, Doran & Co., whose patience and courteous interest have never varied while these slow pages have been unfolding; to Mr. Henry M. Faxon, whose kindness made possible a quiet study when in town; to Miss Abbie Bradley and Mr. S. G. Kimpton, gardener at Bradley Hill, for both herbs and herbal advice; to Mrs. Mary B. Young for her kind gift of many a New England rarity; to Mr. and Mrs. F. Morton Smith for their winter hospitality to my tenderer plants; to Miss Mabel Davison for her unfailing encouragement; to my mother for much good counsel, and to all the good company of fellow herbalists who have helped me with their wisdom and experience.

HENRY BESTON

CONTENTS

ILLUSTRATIONS

HERBS AND THE EARTH

I

OF HERBS AND THE EARTH

It was a pleasant fancy of the ancients that the lights of heaven, the sun and the moon, the errant planets and the military and ordered stars sang each his song as they moved in harmony upon their paths, ennobling thus the shell of space with music. Were mortal ears prepared to sustain such melodies, it was thought, one might chance to hear, at cloudless noon, in a high and quiet land, a sound of the great cry of the sun, and by night and the moon another music not of earth brushing against earth and the blood. In this celestial harmony what song, then, sang the earth? What vast and solemn music did this our planet make as turning upon its poles it wheeled through the universal void rolling up its cities to the sun and its fields down to the night? Was the sound but the unconfused and primal voice of the planet welling forever from its cores of stone, or did a sound of rivers and many oceans, of leaves and immeasurable rain mingle to make a mysterious harmony? And might a listening god, perhaps, have heard echoes of man, the shrilling of a plough turned from earth into earth and stones, or a woman singing her dream and her content?

It is only when we are aware of the earth and of the earth as poetry that we truly live. Ages and people which sever the earth from the poetic spirit, or do not care, or stop their ears with knowledge as with dust, find their veins grown hollow and their hearts an emptiness echoing to questioning. For the earth is ever more than the earth, more than the upper and the lower field, the tree and the hill. Here is mystery banded about the forehead with green, here are gods ascending, here is benignancy and the corn in the sun, here terror and night, here life, here death, here fire, here the wave coursing in the sea. It is this earth which is the true inheritance of man, his link with his human past, the source of his religion, ritual and song, the kingdom without whose splendour he lapses from his mysterious estate of man to a baser world which is without the other virtue and the other integrity of the animal. True humanity is no inherent right but an achievement; and only through the earth may we be as one with all who have been and all who are yet to be, sharers and partakers of the mystery of living, reaching to the full of human peace and the full of human joy.

Here in this pleasant arbour by the herbs, with the grape overhead, and Basil in flower in the open sun, here in this quiet varied with an early summer sound of country birds, one may well muse awhile on how the soul may possess and keep her earth inheritance. The age in which we live is curious and bewildered; it is without a truly human past and may be without a human future, and so abruptly it came that one might imagine some cosmic spirit or wayward daimon to have reached down of a moment and plucked man by the hair. It has lost the earth, but found (since the comfortable century of philosophers in dressing gowns) a something which it calls "nature," and of which it speaks with enthusiasm and embalms in photographs. It has lost as well the historic sense, the poignant and poetic recognition of the long continuity of man, that sense within our hearts which is moved by a chance print in an old book of a countryman ploughing with oxen beside ruins overgrown with Fennel while to one side women clap cymbals together to calm the swarming bees.

A garden of herbs need be no larger than the shadow of a bush, yet within it, as in no other, a mood of the earth approaches and encounters the spirit of man. Beneath these ancestral leaves, these immemorial attendants of man, these servants of his magic and healers of his pain, the earth underfoot is the earth of poetry and the human spirit; in this small sun and shade flourishes a whole tradition of mankind. This flower is Athens; this tendril, Rome; a monk of the Dark Ages tended this green against the wall; with this scented leaf were kings welcomed in the morning of the world. Lovely and timeless, rooted at once in gardens and in life, the great herbs come to the gardener's hand our most noble heritage of green.

2

A garden is the mirror of a mind. It is a place of life, a mystery of green moving to the pulse of the year, and pressing on and pausing the while to its own inherent rhythms. In making a garden there is something to be sought, and something to be found. To be sought is a sense of the lovely and assured, of garden permanence and order, of human association and human meaning; to be found is beauty and that unfolding content and occupation which is one of the lamps of peace.

Gardens today seem often enough neither to seek nor to find. They make their effect, they attain a perfection, and they are curiously empty of human feeling or emotional appeal. In character they are pictures, painted with flowers as with oils, a colour being touched in here and a blossom there till the canvas is ready to be seen. So purely an objective appeal, however, touches but one small and sometimes rather childish side of us, and the methods used to forward it tend to disrupt and destroy the garden sense of order and abiding loveliness. What human meaning have for us these tableaux in the crinoline grand manner, these huge scenes made from everything under the sun, or this use of boorish weeds in a new and unholy splendour, rarities as outlandish as a savage with a skewer through his nose, and old favorites turned hideous by a destruction of proportion? Surely a garden angel with a flaming sword is needed at the entrance of the catalogues! The gardening ancients were more wise. Flowers for them were but an aspect, an incidental loveliness of something near to man, living, and green. Plants were identities, presences to be lived with, known, and watched growing; they were shapes and habits of leaves, powers, fragrances, and life-familiars. A sense of form gave the garden its tranquillity, and one might hear there, in the full of one's own peace, the serene footsteps of the year.

Even such a garden one still makes of herbs. A plant of Balm, lifted from the June earth with its beard of delicate roots, a bush of Thyme in flower in the hot sun, Angelica rising in Gothic reeds where the rich and level earth long stores its rain, each of these is still a use, a potency, and a name. A garden of herbs is a garden of things loved for themselves in their wholeness and integrity. It is not a garden of flowers, but a garden of plants which are sometimes very lovely flowers and are always more than flowers. It is a garden of colour seen as a part of garden life and not as its climax and close, of the pleasures and refreshments of fragrance, of the fantasy and beauty of leaves, of the joy of symmetry and design in nature, of that neglected delight to be found in garden contrasts and harmonies of green. Sweet Bush Basil with its plum-coloured bracts and branches, green leaves and tiny rose-white flowers, Sweet Basil with paler green leaves and whitish florets, Wormwood green and gray, Rue with its moonlight colour of blue-green, Clary with its fine spike of flowers, Marjoram of the enriching fragrance, how empty any garden seems where they have no part! Where there are herbs even the smallest of gardens has a human past and is a human thing. But let there not be too many herbs. The herbalist-to-be must a little beware of a very old and very new confusion.

3

In the fifth scene of the fourth act of *All's Well that Ends Well* there is already a dispute about herbs. Says the Clown to Lafeu, speaking of the Lady Helena, "Indeed, sir, she was the sweet marjoram of the salad or, rather, the herb of grace." To which Lafeu replies, "They are not pot herbs, you knave, they are nose herbs!" The Clown makes answer that he is "no great Nebuchadnezzar" and "has not much skill in grass," but he need not have been apologetic. Nose herbs, pot herbs, salad herbs, and healing herbs, who indeed shall say just which is which and what is what when herbs are confusingly now the one, now the other, now two or three at once, now often enough all four? Bearing in mind, however, that the use of herbs and the manner of this use is all a matter of taste, these groupings are helpful. One may well have one's own corner of nose herbs, a corner of salad herbs, and all the others, but do not be aggrieved if a fellow gardener insists on rearranging everything and shows the captious spirit of Lafeu.

So much for one first confusion; a second is more fundamental. After all, what is an "herb"? In the new enthusiasm for the plants, there are those who will call anything an "herb" from a carrot to a night-blooming Cereus, and put it in their gardens. Horticulture and Botany, holding to a usage familiar to the King James, classify as "herbs" all plants which are not truly shrubs or trees; the dictionary calls an herb "a plant with a use." For lovers of herbs the word has another and much more living sense. In its essential spirit, in its proper garden meaning, *an herb is a garden plant which has been cherished for itself and for a use* and has not come down to us as a purely decorative thing. To say that use makes an herb, however, is only one side of the story. Vegetables, quasi-vegetables, herbal what-nots, and medicinal weeds are not "herbs" and never will be "herbs," for all the dictionaries. It is not use which has kept the great herbs alive, but beauty and use together. Clumsy food plants, curlicue salad messes and roots belong in the kitchen garden, in the *jardin potager*, and not with the herbs. They spoil the look of an herb garden, taking from it its inheritance of distinction; they confuse it; they destroy its unique atmosphere. Fancified horticultural varieties of floral herbs, near-herbs, and herbal relatives which have never been used as herbs—these, too, in general ought to be avoided, and if used, used of climatic necessity and used guiltily. No garden of herbs, moreover, should ever be intruded upon and prettified by non-herbal flowering plants, for such an intrusion destroys the unity and character of the garden, and if one wants bloom there are plenty of flowering herbs.

In making the garden, the emphasis should always rest on the beauty and character of the plants and never for a moment on the size and variety of the collections. Collections of herbs are interesting, often enormously so, but their rivalries end in their becoming much alike, and a fashionable scramble for rarities is not for the herbalist. A garden of herbs is something else, something a little apart from the need of numbering and counting and completing which is in the blood of our years, something which is of earth and of time and of magic and of peace. Let the garden be small and secret if it will, if it be made with understanding it shall gather in its leaves that which has no garden bound or measure.

4

It is the very early morning, the house is not yet awake, and in the garden refreshed with night the bees are working in the herbs. The frailer spikes of Hyssop sway under their weight, bending over like birches swung by boys; the Marjoram shakes and nods to their fumbling and climbing and alighting; on the spikes of Basil they thrust their whole heads into the larger flowers and drive off newcomers with a buzz. Herbs bring bees, bees with their immortal air of fable and the golden age. Labiate flowers please them, for the honeyed reward is generous and kept sheltered for their taking.

Two great botanical families, the Labiatae or Mint family and the Umbelliferae or Parsley family, share between them the majority of the familiar herbs. The Labiatae form a large and strongly marked natural order especially abundant in the Mediterranean region; to it belong the Mints and the Sages, Basil and Balm, Marjoram and Rosemary and Lavender, Thyme, and a scatter more. Plants of this family have commonly a squarish or four-angled stem, simple and opposite leaves, two-lipped flowers springing from the axils of leaves—sometimes arranging themselves there about the main stems in a pretty ring or wreath of bloom—and stamens by fours. Many are fragrant and aromatic, the odour having its origin in a volatile oil stored in tiny glands in the tissues of the leaves. Cereals apart, no single great

BASIL

group of plants has probably been of more service to mankind.

The Umbelliferae or Parsley family are again a large and valuable order. Here belong Lovage and Dill, Angelica, Parsley, Coriander, the Fennels and their like. In this order the individual flowers are small, even minute, and situated at the extremities of little stalks which branch out from the end of a stem (as in the too familiar Queen Anne's Lace) to form an "umbel." Leaves are seldom simple, but cut and divided; and their stalks tend to widen to a sheath at their base to clasp a hollow and rounded stem. Petals are five and stamens five, and the umbel as a whole is often white or yellowish. The aromatic elements are richest in the "seeds" or fruits, but occur as well in the substance of the plant. Umbelliferae vary a good deal in character, some of the species being among the most valuable food plants, others, like the Water-Hemlock, being poisonous.

Rue belongs to a family to which it has given its own name, the Rutaceae; Costmary, the Camomiles and the Artemisias are Composites; Borage and Comfrey belong to the Boraginaceae, and Burnet is of the Rose family.

Collecting herbs and the seeds of herbs is in itself a spirited and complete adventure. Seeds of the rarer herbs are not to be had at every corner. They hide in rare and fantastically interesting catalogues (blessèd for reading in bed), they lurk in the coat pockets of fellow herbalists, in *petites annonces* in French agricultural papers, in small envelopes from Switzerland numbered and hand-lettered in violet ink, and in teacups which have lost their saucers in the kitchens of old farms. In the British catalogues some are entered among the flowers, others in the general list of herbs; the French list a few among the *graines potagères,* a few with the flowers, and put the group as a whole in their medico-herbal muster of *plantes officinales et condimentaires.* So much for the unusual; as widely varied and delightful a garden as one could possibly wish can be made of seeds and plants easily procurable in America. Two or three of the larger firms now carry a good list of herb seeds and offer a selection of plants as well. One nursery makes of herbs a pleasant specialty.

Some day, perhaps, a lost herb or two will come again into human life. Who will bring us from Cretan hillsides an herb known to the Elizabethans and the Victorians, the ancient "Dittany" of the Greek Anthology (*Origanum Dictamnus*), a lovely and fragrant plant long ago dear to gods and to earth-wandering men?

5

Now sweeps a high wind over the farming land, shaking like a banner the fields which today await the mower, rushing wayward this way and that through the fruiting grass, all in a long lashing sound of wind and leaves. The sparrows who have come to glean in yesterday's greener stubble hold close to the earth, their brownish groups fly low, but the higher swallows are caught by the wind and soaring are blown about; the processional clouds move white. What winds shall blow, fall what lustral rains that the ancient sense of the beauty and integrity of the earth shall presently reawaken in the indifferent blood? Or must some great and furious storm (and such storms come) sweep clear the whole coast of the soul of man and restore him thus to his humanity? For man is of a quickening spirit and the earth, the strong, incoming tides and rhythms of nature move in his blood and being; he is an emanation of that journeying god the sun, born anew in the pale South and the hollow winter, the slow murmur and the long crying of the seas are in his veins, the influences of the moon, and the sound of rain beginning. Torn from earth and unaware, without the beauty and the terror, the mystery and ecstasy so rightfully his, man is a vagrant in space, desperate for the inhuman meaninglessness which has opened about him, and with his every step becoming something less than man.

Peace with the earth is the first peace. Unto so great a mystery, to paraphrase a noble saying, no one path leads, but many paths. What pleasant paths begin in gardens, leading beside the other great mystery of nature, the mystery of the growing green thing with its mute passion and green will. The day's high wind is walled off from the herbs, only the taller leaves stirring a little in the fringes of the gusts, the sun mounts from the southeast into the south, the black and yellow bees continue their timeless song. Beautiful and ancient presences of green, dear to man and the human spirit, let us walk awhile beside your leaves.

II

OF TEN GREAT HERBS

The house is part of a farm and is old and country-like and painted a farmhouse red. It stands in the midst of fields on a hillside sloping east, with a lake below lying blue, and north and south are glimpses of the lake again over fields and trees, with hills and farms on the other side, and a far country of woods. On the side of the house overlooking the lake, there is a kind of rustic court, and this is not painted red but white, the change of colour being a custom of the country. Two sides of this retreat are formed by the house itself with its windows and green blinds, a third is provided by an adjoined shed and lengthened by a copse of cherries, the fourth is open to the sunrise and the lake. It is a pleasant and Virgilian place, much loved of birds. One great old apple tree, beautiful in the antique manner, is the rustic guardian of the scene, attended to one side and a little below by an equally ancient pear. In this shelter of green and white, framed by the darker red, in this garden whose floor of grass slopes gently down to join the summer hay, I have my herbs.

There are two borders or beds or gatherings (I am not sure which word to use, for it is all quite unpretentious), one on the north by the cherries, which faces the southern sun, one on the west below an old foundation wall. I take a particular pleasure in this wall for the rustic beauty of its making, esteeming it a small masterpiece, no less, of the old New England art of stone, that folk-art of boulders and field rocks and fragments under the plough which can make even a cellar wall here a thing of beauty and integrity. Only oxen, I think, could have lifted these huge shales lying flat, or those weights of granite whose sides have so frosty a glint of quartz under their weathering. The wall is some eighteen feet long and about four high, and most of the stones are of an archaic greenish grey. Things do well at its foot, for they have its shelter and the moisture it holds in the earth. There Balm lives, growing as Balm should grow in a mass of flourishing, close-gathered green, Applemint made of more interest with a plant or two of its variegated form, Bee-Balm white and red standing close against a corner of the wall, Bergamot Mint with its French and eighteenth-century elegance, English Pennyroyal, the prostrate form, creeping out from under a stone, and a few small plants of Dill. In the longer border facing south grows a whole "tussie-mussie" of plants which have filled out and grown together to make a pleasant and unstudied show. Here are Hyssop and Basil, a corner shrub of Southernwood, a clump of kitchen Sage, Pot Marjoram and Lavender (that European-minded plant), Virgil's Cerinthe with its yellow blossoms, Spike Vervain (to the classical peoples the most sacred of all growing things), a plant or two of the Biblical "Hyssop" which is a Marjoram (*Origanum Maru*) sent to me by a scholar in Palestine, a good clump of Costmary and its botanical relative Camphor Balsam, Lovage and Woundwort, Valerian and Comfrey, a noble plant of Absinthe Wormwood, and even, O happy rarity, that preëminent plant of folklore, the screaming Mandrake Root. The Thymes are by themselves, and to one side and out from the shadow of the northern wall stands that ancient potency, a bank of Rue. A border facing north I give over to a white Astilbe and a very unpretending show of white and yellow annuals.

I write down only those herbs which come to my mind, not wishing to begin a catalogue. Counting almost as I write, with that separate part of the mind which seems to do so well by us at a pinch, I find that I have at the moment forty-three herbs. Of a number of these I keep but one strong plant, which is enough, of others two or three, of those which are used a good deal, six and more. It is a mistake, I think, to have more than forty or fifty herbs at any one time, for the plants are, as I have said, individuals and presences, and to overplant means a loss of that civilized pleasure of growing a beautiful and interesting thing and getting to know it well. The hideous delight of the early twentieth century in masses and numbers was a touch of the insect mind, a thing tent caterpillars would have perfectly understood. My own method is to have a definite group of favourites, mostly established perennials, and with this group as a foundation to try a few new herbs every year or some delightful old ones all over again. A good way to begin a garden is to start with a representative selection and let the garden grow naturally from these when the garden and the gardener's mind are ready. But I had best get to my own notion of such a list.

I call the selection, you notice, "ten great herbs" and not "the ten great herbs," which title would provoke an herbal Armageddon of otherwise peaceable and philosophical gardeners, and conjures up the vision of a field strewn with trowels, and abandoned plants and fugitives. I have come to choose these ten because they are all pleasant to work with in the earth, because they are old and famous plants, and because as a group they give a good idea of what herbs can bring to gardening and living. Basil begins the list, then follow in order Marjoram, Balm, Bergamot Mint or French Bergamot (*Mentha Citrata*), Sage, Hyssop, Rue, Spike Vervain, Lovage, and Lavender. Complete cultural directions, the popular and the foreign names, the matter of native American herbal allies, and so forth, I keep for a convenient and separate table. What I should like to give here is a sense of the herb itself and the impression it makes as a plant and a familiar.

2

We have had three weeks, almost a month, of rainless August heat. Last night, soon after the lamps were lit,

I saw the first small drops on the outer darkness of the panes, and presently from under the kitchen floor the faint whisper of water trickling into the cistern could be heard in the silence of the room. This morning, the whole landscape is renewed, and the garden has its own good smell again of rain-wet earth and leaves. The green life of earth is a deeper life than we know, having its roots in touch with the waters under the earth, with those rills flowing unseen out of ledges deep in the ground. It is when the garden is unable to drink its fill from beneath, when the living ascent of moisture from the deeper earth to root earth is impeded, that plants begin to take on that lifeless air and curious, lifeless feel which surface water never quite dispels. In the court a woodpecker flies into the apple tree, making his way through the leaves without a sound; trees, sky, grass, house, herb garden, and flowers all shine together in a sun with a peaceable air, and walking out to see, I notice that the fine-leaved plants are still comfortably drenched whilst those with simpler and entire leaves are already dry.

In a corner by the wall, a plant of Purple Basil stands quite by itself, and with washed and shining leaves makes vital alliance with the light. No herb is more generous of its fragrance, and this morning the rich, clove-like odour hangs above the plant like a small cloud unseen, mingling its refreshment with the good odour of the earth. You may see the wells of essential fragrance on the under side of the oval leaves, where they appear as a cloud of pinpoint dots. I have both kinds of Basil here, the Purple or Bush Basil and the Sweet or Green. Basil is an accommodating plant. Crowd it into a pot or nook of earth and it will not sicken or go queer, shooting off a long ungainly stem to this side and an abortive nubbin to the other, but will intelligently and interestingly readjust its whole scale, reducing stem and leaf and flower in one proportion. In the garden, too, the herb will give you about what you permit, either a pretty little bush-like form with purple wands and purple bracts and lighter flowers, or a handsome plant which is one of the most distinguished of herbal presences.

A fine plant of Basil is first of all a composition in interesting colours, a Tyrian or red plum-purple and a very living green. The purple is in the branches and the stems, the bracts above the flowers and the tufted rosettes of growth-to-be at the ends of the stems; the green is in the leaves. (Plants grown indoors stay much more green.) These are colours of India of which the Basils used as herbs are natives, a liking for pink and green being traditional in Indian art and life. The growth of the plant is strong, vital, and orderly (it is a perennial treated as an annual), and my large plants with their trunk-like stems and rounded growth above often remind me of miniature and symmetrical trees. The French, with their keen sense of form and feeling for fragrance, grow Basil as an ornamental plant as well as an herb, and have developed a dwarf variety of the Green for use in their rather formal gardening.

The Basils I grow stand nearly two feet tall. The flower "spikes" of the Purple, though they are only purple stems (sometimes branches) wreathed like a maypole with a series of purple bracts and rose-whitish flowerets, are nevertheless unusual and full of character. Green Basil, too, is an excellent plant, of a simpler and more open growth than its companion, and has white flowers and green bracts and leaves of a paler, blonder green. In this garden I give a few plants of the Purple all the room they need and mass a dozen plants of the Green in the general border. Culturally, the plant is a bequest of the Hellenistic world, an herb of the warmer climates of the Roman Empire, and has been known and used from the earliest times as a condiment, a fragrance, and a medicine. No herb of all the garden is more used here by the household; it goes into every nosegay, into the salads, into everything made with tomatoes, an alliance with these last having been foreordained. The Green is the best for general culinary use. The name of the herb comes from the Greek noun meaning "a king," and was perhaps given for the Tyrian purple it assumes. During the Dark Ages Basil seems to have been somewhat lost sight of in the West, but with the Renaissance it came into its own again and recaptured the garden and the imagination.

Whenever I walk among the herbs at noon, at that hour when a Spanish country saying will have it that the forces of the earth are at their exaltation of power, I can never pass one of the great Basils in the sun without a thought beginning there of the fantastic wonder of the whole green life of earth. Pivoted upon its share of soil, potent with its intensity of living, symmetrical and predetermined to symmetry, a fine plant of Basil is a form, a gathering together of that mysterious vitality of green whose veins draw up the earth itself, and whose impulse of life is the other side of that rhythm of life stirring with us in our blood. What a passion for life plants reveal, what a body and desire of life dwell in the dark of roots and the hunger under the earth! What will they not endure to live and bear, not surmount of caprice and outrage, of attack and disaster, if they can but lift one flower from the ruin. What a sense of will there is in the vine, in the groping of the tendril, in the ultimate seizure and adherence! Denied the animal resource of flight, an intensity of life is their ark and weapon; fixed upon earth they can but fight death with life. We are not conscious enough in our human world of this other shaping of life beside us, taking little account of its presence and its ways, yet without such an awareness our thought of life must remain a thing of our own firesides where none see beyond the flame.

With Sweet Marjoram one comes to an herb which is a study in the little elegancies and niceties of proportion. It is of the true Sweet or Knotted Marjoram that I write, *Origanum Marjorana* in the Latin. Not a tiny herb at all, or one which grows primly, no other herb that I know has quite the same appeal of scale, the same small, fragrant propriety.

I have five plants here growing by a little cliff of whitish granite which is the side of a stone continuing the greater wall. They came from a nursery, for this Marjoram is again a perennial treated as an annual, and I like to have well-started plants to put into place in June. All summer long I have watched them growing from thrifty seedlings into charming and very civil little plants of a loosely bushy nature, plants with somewhat red and delicately woody stems, the longer ones curving out and up from the roots, each close trimmed with opposite clusters of small and oval leaves. At the tops of the stems and in the axils of the higher leaves have now appeared the curious and pretty buds which give the plant one of its familiar names. These are the "knots,"

four-sided cones or miniature thyrsi of green whose walls
of tiny overlapping scales thrust from between them the
specks of white that are the flowers. The Elizabethans
thought of them as resembling the heads of boys, and
they do, in a way, recall such a group of clustered heads
as one sees looking out from the corners in the old re-
ligious canvases. The word "knot" itself is undoubtedly
a memory of some device of the old needlework or em-
broidery which the buds chanced to recall.

A neat and pretty plant, Sweet Marjoram is perhaps
the most human and amiable of the smaller herbs. It
is a plant easy to care for and easy to grow; it thrives
in any good garden soil, withstands the vagaries of
weather, and is plagued by no thief of leaves. In domestic use, it is the base of a Marjoram vinegar which is
a pleasant deputy for the Tarragon, and a few leaves—
not too many, for the taste can have a small bitterness—
go with the Basil into salads.

The other Marjoram of which the garden should always have its share (for it is one of the best and prettiest
of the floral herbs) is "Pot Marjoram," call it in Latin
what you will. This is a much heavier, larger plant,
which grows to be a strong, branching clump two feet
high covered with dark leaves and abundant clusters two
or three inches wide of purplish flowers which bloom
all the summer long. I find it one of the most sturdy
and resistant of all the garden plants. It is quite easily
grown from seed, though what you will get depends on
the nursery and your seedsman. It may be *Origanum
Onites*, an old perennial plant from the Caucasus, or
a horticultural variety of the wild Marjoram of Europe
and the British Isles, *Origanum Vulgaris*, a hardy perennial there and a reasonably hardy one here. Practically

all the plants I have seen lately are nursery strains of the *Vulgaris*. Whatever or whichever it may be, "Pot Marjoram" is a plant for every herbalist and every garden of herbs.

In making their gardens and choosing their flowers, the ancients had a profound feeling for the lovely quality of fragrance. Mile upon mile beyond Augustan Rome lay the rose gardens which provided the city with its favorite flower; the Dark Ages saved for us the herbs, keeping alive in their vast and unpeopled ruin such plants as Spearmint and Parsley, which are so human and old that they are not to be found in nature; the Elizabethan flower and herb lists were an old-fashioned floral vase of pleasant smells. For fragrance is indeed what the past well knew it to be, a refreshment and a strength, a sweet and human pleasure, an exorciser of demons from the body and the besieged and troubled spirit. Subtlest of influences, touching the emotion directly, asking nothing from the mind, it not only wakes in us an emotion of place, but summons up as well a poignant emotion of ourselves as we were in time and the place remembered. The odour of a ploughed field in the spring is like a hand laid upon the heart, having in it all the beauty, the poignancy, and the tenderness of earthly living, all the poetry of the melancholy and ecstasy of spring, of the branch, the new leaf and the warm wind, and the sinking of some last great and solitary winter star.

Part of our delight in the good fragrance of herbs comes from their being in relation to mankind. For some odours are subhuman, being contrived and distilled for insects and such small deer, and others are overhuman, being meant for geni, so overpowering are they and cloying. The fragrance of herbs is a thing of the human scale which lies between. Like all other manifestations of life, it is a thing of change, the scents varying subtly with the growth of the plants, the time of the year, and even the time of the day. There are herbs which are best in daytime, and others which are best in the early morning when even the dew upon their leaves is fragrant. Now and then it comes to pass that an herb will have one fragrance in one part of the garden and quite another elsewhere (Hyssop does this), and plants of the same herb all growing together may have marked individualities of odour. With some herbs, Rue, for instance, there is an under-fragrance which is almost a separate thing.

A nosegay of herbs in a room makes no insistence, but once it has the attention it holds it, and it is beyond all customary experience refreshing. The fragrances are real ones, and not, as so many things are with us, manufactured essences one remove from life. That inauspicious suggestion lurking in modern perfumes of the animal mingled with the floral, as if someone had led a musk-ox through a bed of Nicotianas, is with herbs cleansed from the nose. Bouquets of herbs, moreover, stay fresh an amazingly long time and do not befoul the water. Such a bouquet, too, is always a little more than a nosegay, it is a collection of the beliefs, the wisdoms and the fantasies of our kind remembered in green.

Of all herbal fragrances there is none to my mind more pleasant than that of Sweet Marjoram, of that plant which the French call *"Marjollaine à Coquille"* and put with keepsakes and add to salads.

A swarm of bees leaving the hive, said Virgil, rush

like a dark cloud to "sweet waters and leafy shades,"
and there must the bee-keeper hasten to lay "bruised
Balm" and Honeywort that the sweet odours may de-
tain them. The plant he first recommends, giving it a
Latin form of its Greek name, is "Melisphylla" or "the
Bee-Leaf" and the great first-century herbalist Dioscor-
ides adds that bees do indeed delight in the herb, which
is something similar to the "Black Horehound" and has
leaves with a lemon smell. This is no other than the
Balm of our own gardens, now Latinized anew as *Me-
lissa Officinalis*, and variously called in English, Balm,
Lemon Balm, Sweet Balm, and Balm Gentle. No plant
of the garden has a better classical pedigree, and there
is even a possible mention in the Odyssey. To the ancients a plant of fragrance and a companion of bees,
to the Middle Ages a fragrance and the source of a heal-
ing balsam ("Balm" being but "Balsam" made short),
Balm is now a time-honoured presence whose medical
fame has waned, but whose standing as a fragrance and
an herb of gardens is perhaps higher than ever before.

Though it is pleasant to work with plants in a garden
and bring them to their best, discovering what things
help or hinder them, it is also pleasant to have at hand
plants which may be trusted to do their best quite by
themselves. I know of no plant better able to do this
than Balm. Sturdy, hardy, and vigorous, strongly made
and strongly growing, it tends to its own green affairs,
holding the fortress of its soil with a great bush of root-
lets buried and ramified in a large ball of earth, retaining
its grasp, yet not trespassing. Keeping, it would seem,
to the *via media* of classical tradition, it avoids weakness
on the one hand and strength become thievish on the
other, a habit which makes it a particularly pleasant and

dependable herb. It is a genuine perennial, and emerges
from its root in the spring with a leading stalk or two,
one of which tends to become the main stalk of the
summer plant, thrusting out axillary branches as it
grows which in their turn trim themselves with shorter
branches and smaller leaves. The grown plant is not so
much a bush as a lodge of leafy branches, some erect,
others sloped off, all crisp and clean, all fragrant with
a good and earthy smell of lemon. The white flowerets
stand in the axils of specialized stems, appearing in
calices interestingly arranged as a fan, and the buds are
ivory.

Balm is so pleasant a plant and is used so much here
during the summer as a green fragrance in the house
that I have a whole bed of it in the garden which I
allow to grow together in a not too crowded mass of
green. Quantities of it were used in Elizabethan England to scour the furniture and give it a pleasant smell
when notables were expected; there is a reference to the
practice in *The Merry Wives of Windsor*, Act V, Scene
v. It is easy to grow from seed though a little slow to
germinate, and the young plants well placed come into
full growth their first year. Broken light and shade and
a place in moist earth are the best things for Balm, or
a situation in an east border with limited hours of sun;
direct heat and dry soil will but dwarf it. The herb is
normally from twelve to eighteen inches tall. I space
the plants which go into the bed eight inches apart and
allow single plants established outside to have a full
square foot of soil. The herb is occasionally come upon
as a garden escape in old counties in New England and
Virginia.

I find few things in a garden of more curious interest

BALM

than the relation of light and shade to the shapes and surfaces of leaves. Of the colour of leaves and the primary relation of light to that colour I shall not speak here, for it is the difference in the reflection of the light and the adaptation of the surface to the intricacies of light and shade I would rather call to the gardener's musing mind. A leaf is a subtle thing, being far more than a casual first appearance of form and colour and light. There are leaves which by their shape hold the light as in a cup, others which let it flow from them almost as rain might flow; there are leaves which are mirrors reflecting the sun from a glaze of varnished green, and others which are delicate transparencies through whose living screen the sun passes with a strange and lovely tempering. Here in the garden I have these and a hundred other variations, but it is by the leaves of Balm that I find myself pausing when I chance to visit the garden in the morning when the plant faces the eastern sun. It is a simple leaf, not large when averagely well grown, measuring perhaps two inches from base to point, egg-shaped more or less, and scalloped in a descending rhythm to its narrowing end. Very short, whitish hairs rise from its upper surface, thinly sown and often next to invisible, and the usual colour is a greenish yellow-green. So far, perhaps, it might be any of a thousand leaves: what gives it a peculiar interest is the bold texture and the deep indentations of the veins which make the surface an intricate pattern in relief, each minute enclosure being raised to the higher light of the sun, each vein being sunken to an actual channel of shade. It is the sense of the network of veining (so favorite a device of nature) being again a network of shade, which holds my attention as I walk.

For the shadow is melted there when the sun is overhead, and the veins emptying of darkness become but lines, yet swiftly the veining shadow gathers again, being never entirely absent somewhere on the plant. But all nature is full of these subtleties of light, and nowhere are they to be better seen than on the wings of birds and the surfaces of leaves.

3

This noontime, while the men were resting from the mowing, I saw something very curious happen in the field. The hay had been cut upon our upper slopes and lay drying in the stubble, and further down where the grass had been cut a day before, stood a haycock loosely piled. Suddenly between me and the glimpse of the team unharnessed and our neighbours eating dinner in the shade came a small and local whirlwind which crossed the road like a presence, and began its journey down the slope, picking up the hay. The air in its path was presently a wild shower of new hay tossed fifty and sixty feet high, more flying up as the vortex grew in its motion down the hill. It then took the top from the pile, scattered it over the field, and swept on across the uncut lower slope to the lake, darkened it with a catspaw path and vanished like a djinn from a bottle halfway to the other side. Straws and towsles of hay drifted down from the sky, lodging in the leaves of the apple trees and strewing all the nearer road, and presently all was as it had been or nearly so, and the farm bell rang for the noonday meal.

Autumn is familiarly the season of colour, winter is the season of form, spring the season of texture, and summer the season of motion. Leaves and branches move, casting shadows which move beneath them, the long grass ripples and bends, the brooks slide and divide about the stone, the invisible and warmer wind is in itself a motion more intricate than the winter's front of rushing cold. Today, however, save for the djinn which lately troubled the field, a true country peace hangs in the hot sunlit air, and from the garden I follow with my ear the rattling click of the mowing machine to the end of its swale, hearing then the shout and ho! to the horse and the sound again beginning.

In each far corner of the bed of Balm, its leaves mingling with the Balm yet raised above it, stands an herb whose essential quality can best be rendered by saying that it is the most feminine of all the herbs. It is Bergamot Mint (*Mentha Citrata*) or Lemon Mint, sometimes called French Bergamot to distinguish it from the true Bergamot, which is Italian. In texture this herb is the most beautiful of the mints, being smooth and elegant of leaf, the whole plant, indeed, having very much a finished and a measured air. Its leaves are smaller than the leaves of Balm, its neighbour, and the new growth at the ends of the main stems and the axillary branches makes flat and patterned rosettes firmly attached and coloured from below with a bronzy purple staining through with the light to the upper surfaces. Delicate, valid, and in a certain way elaborate, the herb is in general form an outward-growing and loosely symmetrical clump which reaches a height of some eighteen or twenty-four inches. A great favourite in eighteenth-century France, when taste and fashion were of feminine inspiration, it was often included in the flower paintings of the time for the sake of its leaves flushed purple under green and the French violet of the flowers. It still flourishes there in the gardens of old provincial country houses, honoured both for its fragrance and for its use in the making of liqueurs.

As a garden plant, Bergamot Mint needs moist soil and broken shade—more or less what Balm requires—and though reasonably hardy it should have some protection through the winter. Plants are purchasable from American dealers.

Because the violet spikes of Bergamot Mint are not in a conventional sense considered "garden flowers" I find myself pausing a little at the phrase to weigh its meaning. A garden flower, I suppose, is a flower planted for its beauty, or more truly for its aspects of beauty, for we must take our garden pleasure now in a colour, now in a texture, now in a form, now in a fragrance, now in a combination or a partial combination of these elements. The single dahlias blooming at the kitchen door are an example of my meaning, they have texture, an arresting and lovely colour, and a country vigour, and with these they must say their all. An ideal garden flower therefore might seem to be one in which all aspects of beauty were harmoniously united, but the truth is that many very beautiful flowers do not move us at all. Leaving the physical aside, there is another world of values by whose standards we consciously and unconsciously judge the fitness of a flower, remaining unmoved by it unless it awaken some human emotion, stirring some old memory or touching and arousing the imagination. The values of the gardener's spirit are as great as the values of the gardener's eye, and it is because they have been a little put aside that the vulgar curse of giantism has so descended upon us, and gardens have fallen into so impersonal a rut. The lovely spikes of Bergamot Mint are not large, and they have not that importance proportional to their leaves which flowers often seem to need, but they are ringed with colour to their tapering cones, and are fragrant with the fragrance of the herb. They do not *sauter aux yeux*, but they have charm and the power to move the mind, for these same delicate spikes have stood in floral vases in the great eighteenth-century rooms, and heard the urbane delight of music, seen candles brought in to light the brocades and the sword hilts and the jewels, and heard the sound of women's voices discussing the policies of kings.

A little in the shelter of the robust Pot Marjoram and placed near the Lavender stands an herb with as interesting a leaf as the garden shows. In color it is a dull, unvarnished green; in form, an elongated and tapering oval held on a stalk its own length; in texture it is pebbled like the skin of a chameleon. I know of no other leaf which by pure texture gives so curious a suggestion of a kingdom on the other side of nature. Touched with both beauty and strangeness, the leaf is a thing to catch the eye and to prompt a question; it is the leaf of Garden Sage, the *Salvia Officinalis* of the botanists.

I had thought when I put the plant into the garden that friends would quickly recognize it there, but only a few have done so. Apparently Garden Sage as a plant is not as well known as its virtues and uses indicate. Yet the herb is one of the greater ancients, having never lapsed from favour, and its pebbled leaf alone would make it an interesting thing. In its native region of the Mediterranean littoral of Europe, Sage is a true shrub; north of its range it is a garden perennial, throwing out

SAGE

new branches and branchlets every year from the woody base of its stalks. Well-established plants are so easily to be had from dealers that I usually buy mine, taking care to put in a few new plants every other year, for Sage, like many perennials of its type, tends to run out. As a garden plant, I find it one of the most satisfactory of herbs. It is strong-growing, resistant to weather, un-plagued of insects, has something of a flower, and is pic-turesque in color and manner of growth. I put my plants in fairly close together to get a mass effect of the curious leaves, standing them in the full and open light. Sage never looks better, I think, than when I come upon it in the early morning and find the pebbled leaves silvered over with a summer dew. In its way there is nothing more quietly individual in all the garden. Several forms and varieties of the genuine herb are accessible (a form with reddish younger leaves being familiar in England), but American dealers generally keep to one kind, a vig-orous, large-leaved type well suited to our climate. In earlier times the magnificent annual sage *Salvia Hor-minum* was also used in Europe as an herb, and seeds of it and its decorative hybrids are still offered in French and English flower catalogues; I have known it to be called "Annual Clary."

Whatever Sage may have been in the past, and its Latin name shows that it was a plant of saving and heal-ing, it is now essentially a culinary herb. Its place is be-side the spices and the flavours, the condiments and the relishes for which men have risked their lives, fought romantical battles, and committed every form of piracy and sea-rascality known or imaginable in the seven-teenth century. What a curious history could be written of the great spices and the changing tastes in food! The herbs provided cookery with its earliest flavours, and to these the Romans added the Eastern spices (for they had them as they had many of our rarer fruits and table luxuries), experimenting in the sated years of the empire with flavour upon flavour, even adding animal essences to their more fantastic dishes. With the breakdown of the trade routes and the universal poverty, the Dark Ages returned to a native European cookery with simpler flavours, doing what they could with herbs and the clove of garlic, with the onion and the spoonful of wine. It was the Renaissance which took to spices again, having rediscovered them and the East, and the Elizabethans with their usual exuberance filled with spice everything which appeared upon their tables. One familiar dish remains of their cookery, the very typical Elizabethan mixture of meat, spices, apples, brandy, and what-not, which is the mincemeat of mince pie. Though herbs were never entirely disused or disdained, it was the French and the Latins, generally, it would seem, who rediscovered and properly reëstablished them in polite cookery during the seventeenth and most experimental of centuries. Sage was one of the first kitchen herbs of the new dispensation, having been forsaken by medicine, and with the canisters it has stood ever since, an amiable household presence to this hour.

When the heat of some long summer day has followed the sun behind the pasture hill, when the glare has gone and the hour of the garden hose and the watering pot approaches with the dusk, when the whole of nature surrounding the gardener as he works is vibrating with a heavy-laden summer immediacy and profusion of life and there is a moment's flutter of birds in the apple tree, when the lake, the garden, and the hill are each released from the weight and the splendour of day, how pleasant it is to be busy with the earth in this place of green! Here the first coolness comes, welling from the earth and fragrant with herbs, the odours mingling and strengthening as the gardener stirs the beautiful and timeless leaves, here gathers the first quiet of the coming evening, that quiet of summer and beginning night which overlies the fruitful tension of the earth. The herbs tonight approach their summer best, the great umbels of the Lovage breaking into yellow bloom, the tops of the Borage opening their pendent stars, and the spikes of Hyssop like Aaron's Rod ringing themselves with flowers.

Be it the close of a burning afternoon or some cold daybreak of the earlier fall, the Hyssop takes earth and its weather as they come. The garden has no more quietly dependable and satisfactory border plant. A native of southern Europe, and an "evergreen" of the Mediterranean type, it makes no protest at months here under the snow, and emerges sound and vital in the spring; neither dry weather nor the autumn rains in the least bedevil it, and it can be transplanted as casually as one moves a chair. Yet it exhibits none of the truly daimonic fury of vitality stirring in many a hardy plant; it manages things in the other way, living from a deep reserve of endurance and vital power. In appearance an older plant of Hyssop is a kind of little, rounded sub-shrub somewhere from nine to twelve inches high, with branches bushing out from the root and growing erect, most of them branching again. The small willow-shaped leaves occur in whorls spaced along the stalk, each whorl accompanied by axillary tufts of leaflets, and the axillary flowerets borne on the higher spikes are sparks of a vivid violet blue—a white-flowered form being also in cultivation. Younger plants are herbaceous in nature and less bushy in appearance.

As I have elsewhere written, the odour of the herb varies, it being one of the herbal and medicinal smells more than a fragrance, but the general impression of it is of something clean and aromatic with perhaps a very mellowed touch of turpentine. This odour of turpentine (the word is all that is left of the Terebinth tree of poetry) and a lemon fragrance appear again and again in nature. The medicinal suggestion is not misleading, for an old-fashioned syrup made of honey mixed with an infusion of Hyssop leaves and flowers is still in domestic use as a cure for coughs and colds. Hyssop should have a pleasant and sunny situation and the usual good border care. It is the plant we should use for some of the uses of Lavender, for it looks well with other things planted against a wall, and can be used as a pretty and rustic edging for beds along a walk. I have my plants in a row about halfway back in the border with young bushes of Rue before them and Spike Vervain behind.

Hyssop is a pleasant and useful plant, and one with which newcomers to herbs will quickly feel at home. Gardeners with herbs grow into a very living relation with the garden they tend. Their plants are individualities, some more than others, and they come to know them leaf by leaf and quality by quality, taking pleasure in them for the beauty and interest of their garden lives, and content to wait for their changes and manifestations. Impatience does not beset them, for their herbs are of interest from the moment they appear in spring, lifting their fragrance and beauty of leaf out of still another winter; they are willing that their plants shall take their time, well aware that here any flower is but a part of the cycle of beauty. It is from this equable temper of gardener and garden that the living relation between them which can be so subtle and profound can best arise. Only by some such imponderable bond may the response which certain plants make to certain people be explained, the debt on the other side being even more intangible but no less real. When the bond is truly living, both shall be sustained, and in return for the human cherishing, something of earth's patience and instinct of life, something of the peace of gardens, shall find its way into the flowing of the blood.

There is a fine garden scene in Shakespeare's *Richard II*, Act III, Scene iv. It would seem to be about the middle of the morning, and Richard's Queen is wandering with her ladies in the Duke of York's garden at Langley, sorrowful for the trouble of the times, and uncertain where to turn. The head gardener enters with his men, bidding them bind up the "dangling apricocks" and "root away the noisome weeds," and as he and his fellows discuss the garden they point from it a moral of the state of the kingdom, and it is presently said that the King has been deposed. Overhearing the news, the Queen bursts into a passion of angry grief, reproaching the gardener for tidings so unwelcome, and sweeps away, followed by her attendants. When she is gone the gardener soliloquizes, stirred to pity, and ends by saying that where she stood he'll set a bank of Rue, "Rue even for ruth," "in the remembrance of a weeping Queen."

It is only in the world of English speech that this dark and potent plant has come to have an association

RUE

with thoughts of sorrow and regret, and it is all due to a resemblance in the sounds of words. To the Romans, who probably brought the plant into England, the herb was "Ruta," and the name being retained and gradually simplified to "Rewe," a notion of sympathetic identity between the dark leaf and the emotion of "ruth" or compassionate sorrow formed itself in the popular mind. Elsewhere in Europe it remained much what it was in Roman times, an herb and a potency ancient as man himself, a remedy all-valuable and a little dangerous. That Rue could be poisonous to certain skins was known to Pliny and the older herbalists, and I give the warning for what it is worth, for I have never chanced to see a case. No herb has in its way kept a closer alliance with mankind. The ancient nations of the Mediterranean had it from their beginnings, passing it on to the Greeks and the Romans; it stood in the gardens of Charlemagne; it rose dark among the tenth-century herbs; the magic and medicine of the Middle Ages and the Renaissance both acknowledged it as a power; its roots are deep in the folklore of the West. The beautiful name "Herb of Grace" which it still bears in literature is an echo of the times when a brush of it was used to sprinkle the people at the beginning of the mass—the "asperges" ceremony of the Roman liturgy.

Were it ever to come to pass that I could have but two herbs in the garden, Rue would always be the other. There is nothing in the garden more curiously beautiful in its own manner than this plant. Once again, it is a southern European herb, shrubby in growth and a native of its region's poorer soils, in its own countries tending to keep its colour through the year. In the north it grows to be about a foot high, sometimes a little more, coming up each spring like Sage from the trimmed, woody bases of last year's perished stalks. The new growth is dense, the small clumps compact, and in June and July the closely grown tops star over with cruciform yellow flowers like painted amulets. The leaf is as singular as the flower. It is a leaf of fern-like divisions with many rounded lobes, the lesser leaflets sloping in to the central stalk, its substance smooth, somewhat thickened and almost opaque. In colour the plant is like nothing else in the garden, for it is a dark and sombre tone of blue green lightened with a silvering of grey.

I have a few plants of Rue in the border, and a whole bank of it growing by itself in silhouette against the lake. The quality of the herb is best seen when it is given a place of its own; it likes good soil and the sun, and winters best where the drainage is adequate, for the cord-like roots go deep.

Mysterious in colour and strange of leaf, potent, ancient, and dark, Rue is the herb of magic, the symbol of the earthly unknown, of the forces and wills behind the outer circumstance of nature, of natural law suddenly made subject to power. It was with magic that men first sought to control or thwart the wills and the natures of things, calling a cloud with words and forcing back the blood with incantations. Something, indeed, of the great magic of fertility which underlies and overlies religion still lingers on the earth, there to endure till the last child be born and the last field be sown. The instruments of so mighty an art were sometimes humble and small (for magical virtues may choose strange habitations) and power often dwelt among the herbs, in the leaf of Rue, in the spikes of Vervain, there to be plucked and used by the initiate to hold the unknown in the grasp of the known. "Canst thou bind the sweet influences of Pleiades or loose the bonds of Orion?" The herbs are used for magic no more, but the unaccountable remains, like a sound of hidden water in a cavern we have searched from end to end with lights.

4

Here in the North, summer comes earlier to its close, and the sign of the turn of the year is less a first thinning and colouring of leaves than a first great drenching rain. Beginning at night, the small crepitation of the rain wakes the sleeper in the attic chamber, who listens awhile for joy of the sound and is again asleep, the grey morning is confused with rain, and all day long the wind flattens against the house, blowing across the lake from the east and the distant sea. When the weather breaks and the sun again shines, it is autumn. The trees are still in apparent summer leaf, but the substance of the leaves is dry for all the storming, and enough have been blown down to reveal a gleam of the lake through green which was once a wall. It is the lovelier, brighter light of autumn which gilds this seeming summer, the lake is a brighter blue, and a new quiet has come upon the land.

Of what plant it was which first became an ally of man, who shall speak with authority? Was it the wheat with its sacred spear or barley of the dry and fruitful whisper or a wildling perhaps tried for a season and returned again to companions of the grass? One by one, now taken from the wood, now from the river mire, now seized from the barrens and the stone, the plants came into human life, and among the first were the herbs. Was the earliest to come perhaps a magical thing, some potency of earth mysteriously united with powers regnant in nature but not yet become as gods? There grows in the garden here a very ancient plant which has been a part of the magic and religion of the most diverse European cultures, in England being a sacred plant of the Druids, in Scandinavia a plant of the priests of Thor, in Greece and Rome a plant so holy that no other might be used to brush the altars of Olympian Jove. Yet it is not a stately plant but a quite simple one, almost a thing of the roadsides and the fields. "*Hierobotane*" the Greeks called it, the "Holy Plant"; and "*Herba Sacra*" the Romans. To us it is Spike or Herbal Vervain, the *Verbena Officianalis* of Linnæus.

Whatever list of annuals I make for the garden, this ancient herb is sure to be written down. It has enough garden presence of a rustic kind to justify its inclusion, being in no way boorish or uncivil, and it is easy to start from seed and easy to grow. A thriving plant reaches a height somewhere between eighteen and thirty inches, branching loosely as it rises, the leaves being variable in shape but commonly three-lobed, the flowers or florets purple specks borne irregularly on groups of spikes which are elongated and tapering cones. The bluer florets of its native counterpart, *Verbena Hastata*, a taller hardy perennial, are sometimes seen here in waste places, and the plant itself is now being offered by dealers in native things. Seed of V. *Officinalis*, which is still used in domestic medicine as a help in the early stages of colds and fevers, are to be had, as far as I know, only from European firms. The herb is not particular about soil but likes a sunny place, and I have put my plants well back in the border, planting them in a close-growing line, and facing them with some shorter and more compact perennial.

To those interested in magic and religion, there is no herb in the garden more worthy of attention, for this simple plant without fragrance, without an outer look of power, without a flower of significance, was singled out from among all other plants and herbs as the most sacred of the growing things of earth between the Pillars of Hercules and the roots of the Caucasus.

Every herb garden should have at least one of the great perennial umbellates. Standing five, six, and even seven feet tall, the smooth and rounded stems of these magnificent herbs soaring together suggest the lesser pillars which enclose the central pillars of many a French thirteenth-century church, and the foliage is the bold gothic foliage of the tympans and the capitals. With

LOVAGE

Fennel one can plan a Fennel walk in the English manner, standing the plants against a comfortable wall, calling to mind, when the first leaves appear, that over the leaves of Fennel the women wept for Thamuz and Adonis. The strong northern biennial Angelica makes a fine clump, especially when a little individualized, but of these more anon and in their place, for the best of the perennial umbellates is to my mind the bold and hardy Lovage.

Not from the slopes of the Mediterranean littoral, but from the mountains and the plateaus above comes this herb to our gardens, its late Latin and botanical name *Levisticum* being an uncouth corruption of Liguria. Rising in the spring from a very vital and hardy root, it swiftly forms a clump about a foot high of rounded stalks and shining dark green leaves with something of the look and a good deal of the taste of a smooth and handsome Celery. Its stalks thus placed, its first leaves opened, the herb rushes from the ground, the fine hollow columns rising five and six feet high and taking the leaves with them, the great umbels of pollen-yellow florets crowning all. Once used in cookery and domestic medicine, the umbel fruits are now largely neglected, but the young shoots, boiled up in a broth, add to it an interesting flavour of Celery together with Celery seed. The herb likes a situation in rich soil which retains a proper dampness. Hardy as an oak, vigorous in growth, and interesting to the eye, a clump of Lovage is a fine note among the herbs.

I am often in the garden in the very early morning, for I like the quiet, the heavy dew as yet ungathered from the leaves, the quality of the early light, and the smell of earth soon to be mingled with an occasional clean pungency of smoke from the great kitchen chimney. As the garden begins to gather the eastern light, I often come to think that one of the most beautiful and subtle things in nature is the variation of the colour green. There are few things which have a quieter integrity of beauty than the green harmonies of leaves. For some are dark and shining like the Lovage, others pale, each green and each surface making its own byplay with the light; and the greens themselves are rich in variation, ranging from an almost pure blue to yellow. To see both colours upon one plant is a commonplace, for the new growth of blue-green plants is usually a yellow-green. It is by such an economy of means, by such contrasts and transitions that nature varies the entire surface of a world. The silvered darkness of Rue, the fresh green of Basil, and the yellow-green of Costmary are a microcosm of forest and plain, holding the world in a garden as one might hold a leaf in the hollow of a hand.

I once heard from a window on a London street a woman singing the Lavender call. It was not the pretty song so often seen in children's books of music, but another complete and poignant melody, and once and twice and then far-off it rose, touching the heart with its human beauty before it dissolved away into the morning. Something in the soil and climate of southern England, something in the English character, have made Lavender their own, and with it there will always be a thought of its tall spikes against the whitewashed walls of cottages, and of Lavender walks leading from the kitchen garden to the flowers. So cherished indeed is the plant in England, and so many centuries long its garden history, that English Lavender as we know it is the type *Lavandula Vera* no more, but a special and very beautiful garden strain.

English Lavender is one of the really great garden plants. Developed from a Mediterranean form, it grows in English borders to be a handsome shrubby plant two and three feet tall, the leaved shoots rising erect from a contorted main stem and its branches, the leaves *narrow* and grey-green, the spikes comely and rising somewhat above the plant, the flowers a fine tone of the color to which the herb has given a name. This is the traditional "Sweet Lavender," the plant of the herbalists, the gardeners, and the perfumers, the source of the best and most fragrant essences, the herb whose seeds have been used immemorially for linen closets. In France they plant both a French strain of *L. Vera* and a strain grown from imported English seed, together with the broader leaved but less fragrant Lavender known to them as "Aspic" (*L. Spica*). Some botanists, by the way, classify *L. Vera* as a garden form of *L. Spica*, and as such it is entered in various English catalogues, which is a little confusing. With this nomenclature, however, I do not agree, thinking *L. Vera* more probably a separate species. It is not always an easy plant to find. Practically all nurseries here carry "Lavender," but the buyer will receive about as many different kinds of "Lavender" as there are nurseries. Now it is an English horticultural strain of dwarf Lavender, now a tufted broad-leaved hybrid of some mysterious provenance, now a stout cutting of *L. Stoechas* grown in America for rockeries and mingling its faint aroma of Lavender with a hearty smell of turpentine, now the actual *L. Vera* itself, growing with the crabbed unwillingness it manifests in eastern North America.

Outside of California, where any Lavender flourishes, the growing of the herb is an uncertain adventure in American gardens. Every once in a rare while a gardener finds himself confronted with a European-minded plant, a plant which though completely at home in England or in northern Europe, will hardly grow at all in a not very dissimilar American northeast, and Lavender is a typical plant of this kind. *L. Vera* is the best variety to buy, not only because it is the herb, but also because it winters as well as any of the species. Plants which have any chance of flowering should be trimmed in the autumn and never in the spring. Disregarding all horticultural practice, I do not put my plants in a position mercilessly open to our sun, but in a border situation where they are sheltered by adjoining plants and have their full share of broken shade. The Lavender I find most satisfactory, I must admit, is not the herb, but the beautiful species known as *L. Dentata*, a fine Lavender with toothed leaves and tall, symmetrical spikes. Added to the herbs in June, it thrives with the change, coming into outdoor flower late in August or early in September and making a very charming show. Indeed, it is still in bloom when I have to bring it back into the house, for it is not a hardy plant. *L. Dentata* is rather difficult to find, but it is sometimes carried by dealers in unusual plants.

Herbal Lavender was well known to the Romans, who carried on an almost modern traffic in toilet unguents, bath waters, and perfumes, and they would seem to have used it much as we do, making an extract or decoction of it and adding it to the bath. The word "Lavender" clearly goes back through mediæval Latin to the memory of such a usage, for it is related to the classical Latin verb *lavare* meaning "to wash."

I look about the garden, as I close this introductory group of the greater herbs, and wonder what hints and small counsels I might add to help out another gardener? There's Basil: I buy it from a nursery in flats of a dozen plants apiece, it being a little slow to come from seed, not a plant to be handled roughly, for its root system is small and pulls easily out of the earth; there's Balm: if a bed gets to looking crowded, it is best thinned out in the spring; there's Bergamot Mint: a very easy plant to propagate, for its creeping stems will strike root at the nodes when extended along the earth and pegged down with clothes-pins; there's Rue, which roots easily from cuttings; and there's Lavender, which is best transplanted in midsummer.

Every once in a while now as I work in the garden in the late afternoon, kneeling by the herbs and mislaying things and finding them again, some new small bird, some warbler of the inland country making his way down the lakes to the great rivers and the sea, catches the corner of my eye as he moves in the apple branches. A flight of bluebirds has already passed, though I sometimes still hear a bluebird's autumnal call, that sweet clear note with something in it of the plover's tone. The garden has never looked better than it does this very afternoon. The plants are all thrifty, the moisture-loving kinds having taken on a new vigour since the rains, and though leaves may be falling, the old apple and pear remain perseveringly green. The Pot Marjoram is still in flower, the Thymes keep their own midsummer, the Sweet Cicely unfolds again a fern-like leaf, the green of the younger sprays of Balm is as the green of spring.

Surely no plants ever gave so long and lovely a reward. Yet the frosts draw near. Day in the garden now is almost as quiet as the night, and the dark comes with stars and cold. Working here this afternoon, I think to myself that I have only touched upon the rich treasure of herbs, and must presently come to speak of their larger confraternity.

III

OF MANY HERBS OF MANY KINDS

It is winter, and the short-lived and silent day has come to an end over the great landscape of snow, closing at sundown with a sky of frozen pink and channels of clearest green; now clouds and the night make together a greater silence and dark; and snow has again begun to fall. Within the house the lamps are lit, each filled to its brim with oil against the long usage of the hours, and the little parlour is comfortable with yellow light and a wood-stove's fragrant warmth. It is yellow birch which burns in that sable bastille, yellow birch which kindles so readily and whose bright flames send up from chimneys so unmistakable a smoke. And still it snows, falling through the pitch-black and windless night, feathering over the uneven footing of the shoveled paths, ridging twig and branch anew, and deepening the white levels of the lake.

Where the great Basils stood, and the Lavender was put to have its share of the sun, is now all under a good three feet of snow. No longer the wild, beautiful cries of the loon break at strange hours from the lake, on unsettled, rainy days prophesying still more rain; the crows are with us only when it thaws. Jays, who are not often seen or heard here in the summer, are now the most familiar birds, coming to the doors of barns for seeds of fodder which have been shaken from the lofts down upon the snow, and taking to the fence like sparrows when the farm cats pass. The partridges, too, are foraging. There are lilacs by the shed, and late yesterday afternoon, almost at nightfall, as I chanced to pass the huge, frozen bushes on my way to the spring, six of the birds broke from them in a commotion of winged sound, and vanished as by magic into the last of sunset and the luminous darkness on the fields.

A winter evening is the best of times to muse on plans for a garden, for like Bunyan's *Pilgrim's Progress*, gardening is then carried on "under the similitude of a dream." The things we mean to have stand as we mean to have them, thrifty, beautiful, and a pretty tribute to our skill as gardeners; the things we have had, successes and less-than-successes, are something to go on from, are a part of garden history and our lives. On the table, tumbled over the books, on the floor beside the chair, are an armful of the herb-garden plans, catalogues, letters, left-overs, seed packets, garden notes, and general ambitions, and the aromatic scent of herb seeds is already in the lamplit air. Here in this corner, cut from a yellow envelope and sealed with a fold, is more of the Marjoram which is the Hyssop of Scripture, a green papery seed with a dry, agreeable, and delicately bitter smell—the Hyssop of the lintels of Egypt, and of that tragic draught offered and refused. Here is Coriander, rattling like dry rain in its small box, its seeds like chaffy pills, ancient Coriander of the delta of Egypt, first tasted long ago in a child's cake bought at a shop kept by an elderly Bavarian; here is Dill, fresh and pungent; Burnet which comes so readily from the earth; and the flat Angelica seed which tastes of juniper and bites the tongue. But now to garden musings of the winter kind, and a talk of herbs while the fire blazes and the night is young.

2

The growing of a first few herbs is the discovery of a whole new world of garden pleasure and human meaning, but it is when a gardener has tried a few, liked them and been liked by them and would go on that the full adventure begins. Then it is that a preliminary devil lies in wait to urge the eager soul to put in everything which calls itself an "herb," all in the hope of dragging down the garden of herbs into the curious pit into which gardens have so generally fallen. Avaunt, devil, brother to slugs who work in the night like housebreakers, stealing leaves like spoons, and disappearing somewhere out of the night's window, brother to whatever abominable insect it is which bores a hole in the top of a rose branch, seals it above and below, and inserts an infant worm. No, gardener, put in only the real herbs of the human inheritance and only as many of these as you can care for and come to know and cherish, only as many as you can bind into a living relation to yourself, else you will miss the true quality and unique refreshment of gardening with herbs. Should a genuine rarity come your way, take it when you can get it, find a place for it and rejoice —that is understood.

In the following pages I am to discuss a general list of herbs which seem to me worthy of being added to the garden or of making their appearance there from time to time. No authentic gardener could possibly wish to have them all at once, to destroy in a seizure of garden greediness all that the future holds of change and interest. The first ten herbs recommended were Basil, Marjoram, Balm, Bergamot Mint, Sage, Hyssop, Rue, Spike Vervain, Lovage, and Lavender. To increase this first selection of ten to an ampler two dozen, I would now add Thyme, Applemint, Dill, Burnet, Rosemary, Borage, Chives, Costmary, Southernwood, Santolina, Cerinthe, Wormwood (*Artemisia Absinthium*), Sweet Woodruff, and Valerian.

One has to be a little careful with the THYMES. Rock gardening brought in the Thymes in force, and a garden list of them is now so large that it is just another confusion. In a general sense, any form of Thyme may be planted as an "herb," but in a stricter sense the term belongs to a few species with a long garden history: *Thymus Vulgaris* or Garden Thyme, which is the true culinary herb; *T. Serpyllum* or Wild Thyme or Shepherd's Thyme, and *T. Herba-Barona* or Caraway Thyme. The kitchen herb is to be had from nurseries in a "broad-leaved" or "narrow-leaved" strain (the leaves being so small that it makes not the slightest practical difference), and arrives as a miniature bush about four or five inches high with stems like wooden wires and a show of small close-growing leaves. Garden Thyme is an evergreen in its native south of Europe, and like many another European evergreen which has to pull itself through an American winter, it can look like nothing at all in the spring, if it has even survived. Give it plenty of sun, warm, fussily well-drained soil, and keep the little plants together. It can be grown quite well from seed. If the plant grows poorly, one need not split a hair, but search out some plants of *T. Fragrantissimus*, a much stronger little bush and a very pretty one, or of *T. Citriodorus*, another vigorous bush with delightfully fragrant leaves and charming heads of bloom. They should be banked for the winter like miniature roses. *T. Vulgaris*, however, is the true herb, and an interesting presence to know and to have.

WILD THYME (*Thymus Serpyllum*) is the little perennial creeping Thyme which grows everywhere in Europe. There are fields of it on the downs of England, it grows in the gullies of the Channel cliffs, the French Midi is full of it; it was once a part, and perhaps still is, of the ruins and cascades at Tivoli. In France, it is the "Serpolet" of a world of folklore and rustic song; in England, the Thyme of popular legend and Shakespeare's almost too familiar bank. Of this plant famously given to all kinds of variation in form, habit, and colour, my garden contents itself with two varieties chosen for their interest and hardiness: Margined Thyme (*T. S. Aureus-Marginatus*), a form with sage-green leaves edged with a line of ivory; and the type

SWEET MARJORAM

T. Serpyllum with bright, sun-reflecting leaves. The Margined Thyme grows as a tuft, the type *T. Serpyllum* as a woody creeper. Well-drained earth is essential to these creeping and half-creeping Thymes, all of them natives of dry, limestone soils, and our autumnal rains disturb them. Seeds of the *T. Serpyllum* are to be had without difficulty, but it is much better to buy plants. *T. Herba-Barona*, the old caraway-scented Thyme, is harder to obtain, but a bush or two is worth having. English growers usually carry seed.

A plant of Thyme in flower is a delight in the garden. The woody growth, the tiny leaves and branchlets of leaves, the strong Thyme odour strengthened by the sun —all these make it not a plant to stand and look down at, but to see from its own level and with a thought of its own scale. The Thymes are herbs of the classical world, plants of the old agriculture and the gods, the proverbial bee-pasture of husbandry and poetry, the symbol of things cherished and of honeyed and fragrant sweetness. Where they grow, the shadows which enclose the old classical imagery always seem to lift a little, allowing us to see again the farmhouse with its Roman tiles, the spring clearer than crystal, and Soracte white with snow. The Greeks dried the herb and used it to make a fragrant flame at sacrifices, and from this usage and the Greek verb meaning "to offer sacrifice," it has its name.

APPLEMINT (*Mentha Gentilis*) was one of the favorite herbs of old-time New England, and I often come upon it in old gardens in Maine. It is the smallest and neatest of the household Mints, and like New England architecture at its eighteenth-century best, combines restraint of line with social elegance. It comes in two forms, a type-form with red stems and smooth green leaves, and an old garden form with green stems and leaves variegated in green and golden ivory. My simpler form tends to grow as a series of little bushy stalks five and six inches high; the variegated form (which is the stronger, handsomer, and more fragrant) as a little sprawling bush. Both are delightful plants to have, and quite new to all but gardeners with herbs. Stalks of Applemint are perfection for putting into drinks whose delicacy of flavour would be overwhelmed by the stronger Spearmint. The flavour of the herb is the mint flavour with a touch of something unusual added—is it rhubarb? Give Applemint some sun and shade and earth which will not dry out, and take a plant of the Variegated in as a house-plant during the winter. The herb is not entirely easy to obtain, but it is worth the search.

DILL (*Anethum Graveolens*), so familiar as a name and unfamiliar as a living thing, is one of the most beautiful and distinguished plants I think I have ever seen. It is a study in the elements of pure form and the qualities of delicacy and grace, and I always find those who have a living awareness of form in nature curious to know its name. It comes up as a round stem which is at the same time delicate and resolved, and begins to branch simply, the branches being sheathed about the supporting stem, their colour blue-green. Above these branches, above the filament leaves fine as the thongs of the symbolic whip of the Egyptian overseer, appear the great double umbels which are five and six inches across when the plant is strong and well grown. The flowers are only dots of an odd yellow at the ends of the umbel stems; it is the umbel itself as a form which is so fine. A quick-growing annual, Dill comes readily from seed. I sow a row or two in a flat, prick out the half-dozen strongest seedlings, and put them in the border where they can have shelter from the full force of the wind.

Dill is in wide and living use. The northern European peoples have a great liking for it, and in Finland, and in Norway and Sweden, it is grown on every farm. Broken up a little, the tender and unripe umbels are excellent in an occasional salad, and the ripe seeds can be kept for the tops of cakes and for making a Dill vinegar. Dill is a plant of the old "witchcraft," of that curious fertility religion which had a separate life of its own during the great ages of the Church and was finally exterminated in the later Renaissance, having become debased. It is a plant of Pan become Lucifer but still keeping his hoofs and horns, a plant of the god who cannot create out of the void but only out of a created world, and who shakes all things with the earthly ecstasy.

BURNET (*Poterium Sanguisorba*) seems little known in America, yet it is a pretty and very usable herb. One of the most vigorous of seedlings, a plant of Burnet grows from a central root, lifting up its pinnate leaves and edged leaflets till it becomes a fountain of green, some four or five inches high. The flowers, which are only a kind of catkin or cloverhead, should be kept cut out while the herb is in use. Here Burnet serves as an edging and as a grace of the salad bowl. The leaves have a fresh leafy taste of cucumber and are very pleasant mixed in with the lettuce and a scatter of other herbs. Only the younger leaves should be used and these snipped two or three times across with scissors. Burnet may be grown either as an annual or a perennial and grows best and winters best in properly drained ground. To the French it is *Pimprenelle,* and they sow it in dry fields as a fodder plant, and in kitchen gardens as an herb. It is old. The Romans knew it well, and Lord Bacon wrote in its praise.

ROSEMARY, like Lavender, is another exile in our North and East. The herb of remembrance, symbol of memory as tenderness, of loving thought remaining fragrant and green, it is perhaps not entirely unfitting that it should be an exile on our coasts. So profound and moving, however, are its human associations that a garden of herbs must sometime or other come to have it, doing with it what it can. To my mind the best and most civilized way to have Rosemary in the North is to grow it as a house plant which can in summer be put with the herbs. Plants which are not adapted to the seasonal rhythm of North America have to face in our winter a kind of annual murder, and Rosemary is a defenceless, only quarter-hardy Mediterranean evergreen. As a pot-grown plant there are two ways of treating it. The herb usually arrives from a nursery as a small sprig raised from a cutting, and by trimming this sprig and its shoots with judgment and care, a pot shrub or miniature tree can often be grown. A second treatment consists in letting the wandering side-shoots and top-heavy main stem sprawl as they will till the years grow a great coil of fragrance in the bowl of a pot or jar. Horticulture recognizes this second habit and enters a "prostrate" variety of the plant upon its lists.

The herb flourishes in southern England, and again like Lavender, grows magnificently in California. It needs clean, well-drained soil, sunlight, plenty of air, and a disciplined use of water. A few broken fragments of rock from a limestone country are especially good in the bottom of the pot.

BORAGE (*Borago Officinalis*) I plant simply for its flowers. They are star-shaped, pendent, about an inch across, and of a blue which is surely one of the most beautiful in nature. In the whiter, paler heart of each blue star is a massed cone, not of black but of blackish-brown anthers, a colour adjacence of much more interest and subtlety. Such a blue in the ancient magic of colours and symbols was always the colour of the mind as a force: in blue was the divine mind itself reflected. The plant as a whole is vigorous and bristly, its lower leaves being of no value, but the top leaves are sometimes put into drinks to add a doubtful flavour of cucumber. Borage is a plant of honourable antiquity, having been mentioned by Pliny and recommended as a cupbearer of courage and good cheer.

The herb is a quick-growing annual of the easiest culture, attaining a height of about fourteen inches. I sow the seed in a flat, choose my best ten or a dozen seedlings, and put them in the border as a group, a show of Borage in flower being a delightful sight. When not in the herb garden, Borage is an excellent plant to grow beside the peas and beans. Flowers in a vegetable garden humanize it and make it more pleasant to be in and work in. That original combination of morning glories and scarlet-runner beans beloved of the French farmer should be cheerful under our American sky.

CHIVES go in for both gardener and cook. As a decorative plant they have never had their due here, though the Europeans make a great deal of them and catalogue a number of varieties. The large cylindrical stalks, the flower heads like flattened spheres stuck with tufts of lilac, make a bold and interesting show in the later spring. Garden Chives (*Allium Schoenoprasum var. Sibericum*) belong with onions and garlic bulbs to the lily family, and the original plant from which the garden variety is descended grows wild in North America and Eurasia. Give a mat of chives a share of both sun and shade, earth which will not dry out round the fine roots, and cut the flower stalks off close to the ground the moment they are through flowering. Chives are among the hardiest of perennial herbs.

COSTMARY is called "Sweet Tongue," here in Maine, and grows half wild on the edges of old orchards and near old farms. It is a simple and rather rustic herb, "*de plus rustique*," as the French catalogues say of country things, but I have a particular liking for it: it has character. A perennial and of the hardiest sort, the herb spreads from a running root, raising itself up as a stalk or group of stalks thickly clothed with whitened oblong leaves which decrease in size as they ascend the stem. Such flowers as it has are but abortive greenish buttons; the quality of the plant is in the mellow old-fashioned fragrance of its leaves.

Costmary is a pleasant herb. A stalk of it reinforces and accentuates the other herbal fragrances in a clutch of herbs, and the leaves make a slightly bitter medicinal tea. Originally an herb of western Asia, it was probably introduced into Europe by way of Greece, for Greek physicians were intelligently interested in the medicinal qualities of plants. Indeed, the very English-sounding name is of Greek derivation, and freely translated means Balm of (St.) Mary. In Botany the plant bears the impressive designation *Chrysanthemum Balsamita var. Tanacetoides*.

BERGAMOT MINT

SOUTHERNWOOD (*Artemisia Abrotanum*), long a border plant as well as an herb, is still called "Lad's Love" in old-fashioned gardens. It is really a small perennial shrub which puts forth a certain amount of tender aromatic growth every year, some of which is lost during the winter and some retained. The leaves, like those of Dill, are filaments of green. I have just one bush which stands in sun and broken shade and out of reach of the wind. The fragrance seems to vary in quality with individual plants, some having the strong but pleasant herb-and-turpentine smell which the French declare is sovereign against moths, others almost no scent at all. The name "Lad's Love," which has been explained in so many pretty and fanciful ways, is an exact translation of the name of the plant in classic Greek. Nurseries often have Southernwood or can get it. Said by botanists to be a native of Continental Europe, it is probably an herb of temperate Asia as well, for I am told that it is well known in Chinese gardens. Southernwood is a quiet, pleasant, civil thing in a garden, a fit neighbor for Chinese philosophers discussing life and poetry by a pool.

SANTOLINA, for some absurd reason now called "Lavender Cotton," was called "Ground Cypress" by the Romans, a title lately usurped by Kochia, that perfect plant for the entrance to one's garage. It is a pity that the classical name has thus been filched, for it is much the best of the herb's various names, and belongs to it by an honourable inheritance of over two thousand years. What the herb really suggests more than anything else is a little tree a foot high of silvery green-grey coral. It has no leaves in any familiar sense of the word. Once used by the Romans as a medicinal herb and discussed

by Pliny, Santolina is now entirely a decorative plant.
A little bush here and there makes an interesting study
in form and colour, and the coral-like growth has an
aromatic fragrance rather like a milder Tansy. Some use
it as an edging, but I think it perhaps too sharply individualized and conspicuous for such a use, except in a
very formal way. The herb makes no particular de-
mands, asking simply to be put in warm and well-
drained soil and let alone to thrive, establish itself, and
bear its catkin flowers. My plants make cypress-shaped
bushes about a foot high, and I have put them where
they are not swung about by the wind. For a Mediterranean evergreen, Santolina winters unexpectedly well
—only be sure to watch for it in the spring, give it care,
and help to get it going.

CERINTHE or Honeywort will be a new plant, I imagine, to most growers of herbs. It is the pretty yellow-
flowered bee herb of Virgil and the Latin historians of
agriculture; eighteenth-century editions of the Geor-
gics often have a figure of it, the old ink turned brown
upon the brown and ivory plate. Pliny describes it, and
to quote from the notes in an old Virgil, "Philagyrius
says it derives its name from a city of Boetia where it
grows in great plenty." Philagyrius I know not, but
Cerinthe grows well for me, becoming a strong, rather
rustic plant, and its small, bell-shaped yellow flowers
and spotted, alternate leaves are a pleasant feature in
a garden whose flowers are so many of them in tones
of violet and purple. The seed of the herb must be
purchased abroad. Two kinds are usually available,
Cerinthe Alpina from northern Italy and the Tyrol, and
C. *Retorta* from Greece, both perennials. The plants are
considered hardy, but I have not had them long enough

to vouch for that side. A vigorous herb, Cerinthe needs room, good garden soil, and its share of sun. Good plants grow to be about twelve and fourteen inches high.

WORMWOOD is all at once a drug, a symbol, and an herb. A tonic dose of bitters has always had a certain medical value, and "Wormwood" was the bitter of the ancients, being distilled from the leaves of various bitter Artemisias, and especially from the plant *Artemisia Absinthium.* Known to the peoples of the Roman Empire and in wide use, particularly esteemed in the Middle Ages, A. *Absinthium* retained its medical reputation well into the later seventeenth century, and then began to lose it, the plant itself retreating during its eclipse from the gardens of great houses to cottage gardens, and from cottage gardens to the roads. It is now, however, widely grown again, this time as the source of the active ingredient of absinthe and various other bitter liqueurs, "Wormwood" and "Vermouth" being forms of the same word. As a symbol, Wormwood stood for what was bitter and troubling to the soul. One thinks of Hamlet's sullen mumble of "Wormwood, wormwood," as he listens to the player queen's protestations, and of that furious star named Wormwood which fell from heaven across the darkened sky of the Book of Revelation and made bitter one third of the waters of the earth. A. *Absinthium* can with patience be grown from seed, but it is better to get plants which are once again being offered by the nurseries. The herb is grey-green in colour, and the much-divided leaves are silky on both sides; it grows to be two or three feet high and becomes shrubbier as it thrives. I find it a reliably hardy perennial. Slugs have a horrible absinthe craving for its leaves,

and unless held off will eat them to the bone. Another
Wormwood, Roman Wormwood (*A. Pontica*), is often
seen in old gardens of herbs, a vigorous, spreading, grey-
green affair which should have a corner all its own. The
culinary herb Tarragon (*A. Dracunculus*) is the only
one of the Artemisias with *simple* leaves. In buying
plants beware of any with divided leaves, for these are
the "false tarragon" which dealers frequently offer for
the true. A plain, branching plant, it is not much to
look at as an herb, but those who like its flavour can
easily find a place for it as a bit of green. It is a tender
perennial which does not produce seed in the North,
and is propagated by cuttings.

SWEET WOODRUFF (*Asperula Odorata*) is an herb for
a shady corner, especially a corner it can have for its
own. It is a neat and pretty plant, standing six or seven
inches high, the foliage fresh and green, the florets snow
white, the leaves arranged in a whorl about the stems.
It has always been particularly cherished and valued in
Germany. Bunches of Woodruff hung up to dry will
fill a whole attic with a fragrance like new-mown hay,
and dried and seasoned will make an interesting brew
often used by gipsies as a tea. It is a native European
plant and a reliable perennial.

VALERIAN is a garden term which covers the virtues
of two different plants. The true Valerian of medicine
and the older herbalists is *Valeriana Officinalis*, the tall,
strong-growing plant with pinnate leaves, high flower
stalks, and flat, whitish-lilac flower heads seen so often
here in Maine, where it is called "Garden Heliotrope."
V. Officinalis is one of the hardiest and most dependable of perennials, but it is a rank spreader, and perhaps
just a little coarse, so I do not recommend putting it

among the herbs. It is an excellent plant, however, for use in the left-overs of space one occasionally encounters on the frontiers of garden areas, and for establishing in half wild situations. I use it on the side of a path leading into the herbs from the North, and there it walls off the wild growth, spreads to its heart's content, and looks very well.

The other Valerian which is also planted as an herb is Red Spur Valerian or "Pretty Betsy" (*Centranthus Ruber*). This herb belongs to the same Valerian tribe as V. *Officinalis* but is quite another sort of thing, being really a pretty, old-fashioned garden plant with flower clusters of an unusual pinkish red. It is a hardy perennial which will do well in almost any garden soil, but responds gratefully to encouragement, growing about a foot and a half high and continuing in blossom from middle summer into fall. The Valerians are plants of a famous family. The Spikenard of Scripture and the classical authors is a plant of this order, *Nardostachys Jatamansi*. An herb of Butan in India, it was carried by way of Arabia to Asia Minor and thence to the great trade routes of Rome. Valerian is a plant of the old folklore, a protector of house and household from "things which go bump in the night," and children who were afraid to go to bed in the dark were given a sprig of it to put beneath their pillows.

3

So there you have a gardener's first two dozen herbs, chosen and written down on an evening of winter quiet, books, and garden thoughts. The night is still young, shall I run through what is left of my list, saying but

a word or two about each herb? A list it will have to
be, there's no avoiding it, but I trust it will not seem
just another catalogue of herbs, for it is essentially a per-
sonal selection of plants which I have found beautiful,
worth knowing, and last but not least, reasonably available. It is folly to plant vegetables, umbellate "greens,"
garden commonplaces, and herbal duplicates and tripli-
cates when there are all kinds of beautiful and historic
things within reach of our hands. Only one of the really
great herbs is "lost," the beautiful Dittany I have already mentioned, and for that reason I have not entered
it on my working list, nor have I listed the Biblical Hyssop (*Origanum Maru*) or the Mandrake (*Mandragora
Officinarum*), both gifts, and as far as I know not to
be had from any American or European house. The list
to follow includes, I think, the body of any table of
herbs, together with a few which have not yet been discussed. But to the list, perennials it shall be, and no
favourites this time but *a* and *b* by the alphabet.

1. AGRIMONY (*Agrimonia Eupatoria*), an old-
fashioned country herb with a mediæval reputation as
a panacea; flowers yellow and in tapering spikes; whole
plant faintly aromatic; grows one to two feet high;
makes an herb tea. Seeds may be had from French
seedsmen. Botanically related to American Agrimony
(*A. Hirsuta*). A homespun, simple plant, but a tuft or
two of it interesting, best put in a not too conspicuous
place. Cut the flowers after blooming.

2. ALTHEA (*Althea Officinalis*), the country "Marsh-
Mallow" of old-fashioned medicine, grows about two
feet high, has soft, downy leaves and axillary branchlets
of small rosy purple or bluish purple flowers of the
Hollyhock kind. A very old herb, useful for flower col-

HYSSOP

our, easy to raise, not to be confused with *Malva Moschata*. Best seeds from France.

3. ANGELICA (*Angelica Officinalis*), a tall, very hardy biennial growing four to six feet high with a huge umbellate flower and leaves very like celery leaves. Difficult to grow from seed; when trying, get only the very freshest autumnal seed and sow outside a day or two before the ground freezes. Inside sowing of fall seed not recommended to those who have no greenhouse. An herb worth having; nurseries ought to carry it.

4. BAYBERRY (*Myrica Carolinensis*), a native plant so familiar that it is rarely seen with awareness. Well worth having to represent the sweet shrubs. Leaves have a fragrance resembling that of the true Bay with which it was once confused. Bayleaf of cookery comes from a true Laurel (*Laurus Nobilis*); our Bayberry is a Myrtle, and its virtues are esthetic and medical.

5. BEE BALM (*Monarda Didyma*), called "Bergamot" by the English, a native American long naturalized in gardens. Comes in tones of scarlet, magenta and even pinkish-white; get plants of the older strains, as their leaves are better proportioned to the blossom than are the leaves of the newer hybrids; beware rusts.

6. CAMOMILE (*Anthemis Nobilis*), an humble tuft of pretty, fern-like greenery, mildly aromatic; dried flowers make a famous tisane; good for rockwork and a relief from Sedums.

7. CAMPHOR BALSAM (*Balsamita Vulgaris*), an old-fashioned rustic plant with green-grey leaves smelling of camphor; grows from twelve to eighteen inches high; an interesting garden companion to Costmary. Seeds to be had from English growers.

8. CLARY or "CLEAR-EYES" (*Salvia Sclarea*), a fine bi-

ennial sage growing about two feet high; leaves woolly; flowers borne on a spike and cupped with contrasting bracts. Will flower first year, if started early; keep basal leaves protected from slugs. Seeds from England or France. A decoction of the mucilaginous seeds of this plant was used as an eyewash.

9. COMFREY (*Symphytum Officinale*), a large rough plant with a liking for moisture; flowers are interestingly placed. Called "Comforty Root" in New England. Has a long history in popular medicine. Very hardy and well worth having. Not in cultivation, but often found in old gardens.

10. ELECAMPANE (*Inula Helenium*), not in scale with the rest of the herbs, and best put by itself. Resembles a Brobdingnagian Dock with ragged composite flowers; very hardy, and sometimes seen growing as a weed. Elecampane or "Horse-Heal" is the historic herb of the horse-loving peoples coming with them out of Central Asia and going with them and the horse to the ends of the earth. Can be had from dealers in native plants.

11. FENNEL or PERENNIAL FENNEL (*Foeniculum Officinale*), another tall herb of the umbellate type with bright yellow florets and feathery leaves; comes easily from seed; much resembles Dill. Worth trying when the garden is ready for change and variety among its umbellate herbs. Leaves used in salads and as a hors d'œuvre; also as a flavouring in sauces.

12. FUMITORY (*Fumaria Officinalis*), another rustic European herb of country medicine and folklore, botanically related to the familiar "Bleeding Heart"; flowers rose tipped with purple; height about twelve to eighteen inches, a quiet, inconspicuous, rather interesting plant

whose smoke, *"fumus,"* was once thought to have the power of expelling demons. Seeds to be had from France.

13. GERMANDER (*Teucrium Chamaedrys*), well called by the French "Little Oak" from its manner of growth and the shape of its leaves; none too hardy; pretty as a specimen plant or a pot plant, and a distinguished edging where the climate permits.

14. GOAT'S RUE (*Galega Officinalis*), a very ancient plant which has served both as an agricultural plant and as an herb. Has pretty, showy clusters of purplish blue Sweet-Pea-shaped flowers; hybrids now available; grows bushily between two and three feet tall. Seeds to be had from either French or English seedsmen.

15. MONK'S HERB (*Mentha Rotundifolia*), a large, vigorous, sprawly mint with thick stalks and large woolly leaves; smells like Spearmint with a ranker overtone. Was much used in monastic medicine; makes a very fair tisane, as the objectionable flavour does not carry over. Sometimes called "Woolly Mint." Beware leaf-eating insects and caterpillars. Plants may be had from American nurseries.

16. PENNYROYAL, English kind (*Mentha Pulegium*), stems prostrate and creeping, leaves small and oval, a vigorous ground runner, taking root as it spreads; likes a damp situation. Odour resembles that of American Pennyroyal, but is heavier and more medicinal. Makes a tea famous as a remedy for colds. Not really hardy; can be used as a house herb.

17. PEPPERMINT (*Mentha Piperita*), a vigorous hardy Mint of a bushy and rather sprawly habit, but with neat leaf branches and neat leaves. Can be used as an occasional substitute for Spearmint in cold drinks, and dried

for an excellent winter tea. Peppermint of commerce distilled from this plant. A few clumps are worth having.

18. PULMONARIA (*Pulmonaria Officinalis*), or Lungwort, a close relative of our *Mertensia Virginica* and sometimes called "Soldiers and Sailors" from the same two-colour effect of the flowers, has leaves interestingly spotted with white. Was used for maladies of the chest. Various Pulmonarias are offered by French and English seedsmen; *Pulmonaria Officinalis* a little difficult to obtain.

19. SAFFRON (*Crocus Sativus*), an autumn Crocus with a long history as a drug, a flavoring powder, and a pigment, only the golden stigmata of the flower being used. Pretty but capricious as a garden plant, often refusing to flower. Needs winter protection.

20. SPEARMINT (*Mentha Viridis*), probably the most familiar of the perennial herbs. Will grow almost anywhere but has best flavour in the shade; new and tenderer growth can be brought out by frequent cutting. Of this plant the French make their best *infusion de menthe*.

21. SWEET CICELY (*Myrrhis Odorata*), an old herb of the umbellate family with an aromatic and very beautifully divided leaf. Grows to be about two feet tall from a fern-like clump. Difficult to raise from seed. Use same procedure recommended for Angelica. Seeds to be had from England or France. If unsuccessful in raising it, try its close relative, "American Sweet Cicely" (*Osmorhiza Longistylis*), a smaller native plant with the same delicacy of leaf. Can be obtained from dealers in native plants, and is well worth having whether or not you have *Myrrhis Odorata*.

22. SWEET MAUDLIN (*Achillea Ageratum*), another very old-fashioned cottage plant; has yellow flowers and an aromatic fragrance; grows about two feet high and comes easily from seed; makes a third with Costmary and Camphor Balsam.

23. WINTER SAVOURY (*Satureia Montana*), a shrubby herb more attractive as a little plant than as a large one; fairly hardy; said to make an attractive edging where the climate permits.

24. WOAD (*Isatis Tinctoria*), an interesting European plant closely related to our familiar weed the wild Radish; a little coarse in growth; has yellow flowerets on stalks. Famous as the herb with which the ancient Britons used to dye themselves blue. The French call it "*Pastel*" and sell it as a forage plant.

25. WOUNDWORT (*Stachys Betonica* or *S. B. Officinalis*), a rugged clump of heart-shaped, leathery leaves on leathery stems; "heads" of rose-purple flowers similar to the flower heads of the common Prunella or "Self Heal"; very hardy; needs broken shade and moisture in the ground. Offered by various American nurseries. Not a plant for the front of the border, but a good one for shady corners under large plants.

4

The handful of herbs remaining (with the exception of Caraway, which is a biennial) are annuals or plants usually treated as annuals. All are of interest, and three or four are especially worth a trial. A group of umbellates with aromatic "seeds" or fruits, Anise and Cumin, Caraway, and Coriander begin the list.

1 & 2. ANISE and CUMIN (*Pimpinella Anisum* and

SPIKE VERVAIN

Cuminum Cyminum), two very old herbs from the warmer countries of the eastern Mediterranean, Cumin with rose-coloured florets being the more interesting but the more difficult to grow. Sow them both where they are to stand and in a warm position, for both are bad transplanters and need heat. One's luck with Cumin in the North depends a good deal on the kind of summer, but it should do particularly well in the South. Anise grows to be about fourteen inches high, Cumin to about ten or twelve inches. Both are used in the manufacture of cordials and liqueurs. These herbs are interesting for their Biblical and classical background, but are of no great distinction as plants.

3. CARAWAY (*Carum Carvi*), one of the commonest of field herbs here in Maine, having been brought into the state by the Waldoboro Germans in the eighteenth century. Those who have not seen it and chance to like the fresh caraway flavour will find it quick to come from seed, useful, and more of a farm-garden plant than an herb. It much resembles a minor "Queen Anne's Lace."

4. CORIANDER (*Coriandrum Sativium*), the best, to my mind, of these four seed-bearing herbs. It is much the strongest and hardiest, comes without difficulty, if a little slowly, from seed, and the "seeds" or fruits, once dried and rid of their green rankness, can always be used in spice candies and pastries. If given a good start, Coriander grows, to be about two feet high; in sowing it, it is well to face the row due south. When the Israelites murmured for the fleshpots of Egypt and the fish "which we did eat in Egypt freely," they added that the manna which bored them had a taste of Coriander seed. As these four herbs die down rather quickly, it is best

not to grow them near the longer lived perennials or where a "gone" spot in the garden will be conspicuous.

5. CHERVIL (*Anthriscus Cerefolium*), a pretty, fine-leaved herb used in salads. It makes a ferny bed of greenery and tastes pleasantly of Parsley mingled with Caraway. It is easy to grow and worth trying.

6. POT MARIGOLD (*Calendula Officinalis*), merely our Calendula in its small, single, and old-fashioned form, and as such is pretty in a garden of herbs, the great double modern Calendulas having no place there. The best seeds are to be had from England.

7. HOLY THISTLE (*Carduus Benedictus*), a handsome annual from southern Europe once considered a sovereign restorative and still having some reputation, but turn to *Much Ado About Nothing*, Act III, Scene IV, where the ladies Beatrice and Hero discuss Margaret's saying, "Get you some of this distilled Carduus Benedictus, and lay it to your heart; it is the only thing for a qualm." Carduus is easy to raise, and well worth trying some year as a decorative plant. Seeds of it are still to be found in the flower section of the French catalogues.

8. JOB'S TEARS (*Coix Lacrimae Jobi*), a grass discovered in the East Indies during the seventeenth century and with the good imaginative vigour of the past promptly distributed over Europe as a cure-all. Strung on a strong thread, the oddly shaped, pendent seed cases are still sold in pharmacies as an aid to infant teething. The plant comes easily from seed and grows to be anywhere from twelve to twenty-four inches. Well worth more attention from herbalists, as it is picturesque in itself and can be planted as a representative of herbal grasses. The seed is to be had from American firms.

9. PARSLEY (*Garum Petroselinum*), today essen-

tially a plant of the *jardin potager*, but in ancient usage and literature an "herb," and as an herb completely worthy of attention and garden use. Sprigs of parsley are so often seen upon a dish and it has so chaste a union with cold meat, that nobody ever looks at it as a plant or sees that it has beauty as well as function. Yet the Greeks made wreaths of it and decorative garlands, dedicating it as a plant to the gods. I use it here (as it is said to have been used in Greece) as an edging, shearing it and cutting it back at need, and finding it very beautiful in colour and luxuriance of growth, and very living. Parsley is best bought already started in a flat, as it is slow to come from seed.

10. SUMMER SAVOURY (*Satureia Hortensis*), one of the pleasantest of the sweet-herbs, and sooner or later to be tried by every gardener. It grows as a little erect bush about a foot high, and flowers on slender stalks from the axils, the flowerets being a pale lilac in colour. Sow this Savoury early, getting it started indoors if possible, and leaving about five inches between the seedlings set out. The entire plant is of an agreeable aromatic fragrance and may be used in the house and the kitchen in a dozen different ways. It is this pleasant annual which is the true *Satureia*, the plant loved of the Satyrs and grown by them in rustic pots on the window ledges of their shelters in the fields. To these leaves and this fragrance they returned from their flocks and vines, their hoofs drumming upon the sunbaked Italian earth, these little branches refreshed for them the oil and the wine. For the Satyr was once a companion to man and a sharer of the earth, hearing the sudden flutter of leaves by the door and knowing the smell of twig wood burning, a great prophet heard him cry to his fellow, and

long afterwards a father of the church had with such
a one an urbane and distinguished colloquy. This herb
is his, coming to us out of the Golden Age, and the
seed we sow is a little put between our fingers by those
half-human and immortal hands.

5

So closes the garden list, but certain very familiar
herbs were not planted in gardens, but only domesti-
cated in and about the old farms. No housewife ever
planted Catnip with the Applemint and Balm, it was
sown as a "patch" somewhere—"this side of the hen-
house" or "down by the shed" and there left to the cats
and its own devices. How often one comes upon such
patches still, suddenly made aware of the limp, flannel-
like leaves of Catnip underfoot by the strong, accusing
odour in the air. The same thing was done with the
other common herbs of country medicine, the old white
Horehound of England (*Marubium Vulgare*), that wan
nettle-like presence with its pointed, hostile bracts. It
is in such patches that these time-honoured but weedy
herbs still belong; the garden is not theirs. Both are perennials, though the Catnip plants I oftenest see are the
vigorous seedlings which might be annuals and are great
travellers; the Horehound as I remember it holds more
closely to its place. To this day, patches of Horehound
stand back of many old houses on Cape Cod; I often
used to come upon them in the Eastham years.

The old-fashioned country pharmacopœia was a
quite comprehensive affair. Its materials included Indian recipes of powdered roots and powdered leaves,
naturalized European herbs and weeds, and a whole

countryside of native herbs and simples which each household gathered after the crops were in, the secret of their growing places being a sort of family inheritance. Sweet Fern and Wild Ginger, Sassafras and Mullen, Tansy and Coltsfoot, each had its rôle and reputation, and pedlars from the uplands tramped all New England with heavy bundles of the prepared leaves swinging from their shoulders on a yoke. As medicines (when they were not simply harmless and comforting drinks) the infusions were for the most part either mild stimulants or astringents, oftenest the latter. Now and then a "simple" was a powerful drug, such as Digitalis, which came into medicine from an English "wise woman's" garden, but these were rare. Here in New England, Catnip (*Nepeta Cataria*), Thoroughwort (*Eupatoria Perfoliatum*), Pennyroyal (*Hedeoma Pulegioides*), and Horehound were the household favorites among the herbs hanging head downward from the drying racks in the attic; they are favourites to this day. Many a boy has choked over a horrible dose of Thoroughwort about as efficacious as a rabbit's foot, but Catnip Tea was and is a restorative brew to drink when weary, and Horehound and Pennyroyal are still valiant against a cold.

A "patch" garden of the old simples might be a picturesque affair. There one could put the interesting things which have no place with the great herbs and really prefer a free existence. American Pennyroyal belongs here, a plant of the pond shores which does not take overkindly to cultivation, though seeds of it are now on sale; Catnip and Horehound; the Calamints or Wild Basils (*Calamintha Clinopodium* and *C. Nepeta*), wild things both, having practically gone out of use; Wild Ginger (*Asarum Canadense*), an interest-

ing perennial; Wintergreen (*Gaultheria Procumbens*)
which the English have imported for the beauty of its
leaves; Gold Thread (*Coptis Trifolia*)—these last three
sold by dealers in native plants. Here Tansy can go in,
if you want so familiar a weed at all; the native Wild
Mint (*Mentha Canadensis*) with its queerish stick-of-
gum smell; the beautiful but more tender Maryland Dittany (*Cunila Origanoides*); Motherwort (*Leonurus
Cardiaca*), a picturesque weed once used in popular
medicine; and Sweet Flag (*Acorus Calamus*); not culti-
vated things by any means, nor yet ferally wild, but all
touched somehow or other by the hand or the thought
of man. A fancy for including really wild simples will
lead one across Gray's Botany. To my mind the three
most interesting plants of this rather misty group are
Wild Ginger, the Wild Mint, and Sweet Flag. I have
them here and find them all hardy, and the solitary
flower of the Ginger is one of the quaint reassurances
of spring.

But it grows late, half the household is already abed,
the clock pipes its cheerful cuckoo call over a faint whirr
of weights descending, the hour is at hand to give the
house over to darkness and the winter night. Now shall
the billet of oak be thrust into the stove, all night long
to feed a little glow of gnawing flame and keep the core
of the house human and warm, the lamps turned down
and quenched, the doors secured, and the last hand
light carried through the darkened rooms past the silent
and familiar things. It has stopped snowing. The north
has cleared, and beyond the window of a passage the
pole burns blue and cold, touching with the light of
stars and space the garden in its drifts and the snow

pressed like a wave against the wall. And so to bed, taking with me to their cupboard under the stair the lists, the letters, and the seeds, hearing in their dry rustle and slide the promise of a garden.

IV

OF PLANTING AND GARDENING

Any account of herbs would be incomplete if it had
nothing to say of the making and planting of a garden.
The matter of soil is immemorially the first thing to
consider, and with "good garden soil" one is ready to
begin. The phrase is politely vague, but no gardener
needs of it an elaborate definition, and I take it to mean
a soil with a reasonably deep and workable loam, an
undersoil favourable to drainage, and that innate vitality which can never be caught in the symbols of chemis-
try or the frame of an explanation. No soil under heaven
will suit everything unless it be that loam we vicariously
left behind in the first of gardens: we have to do our
best with what we find, and the vast generality of herbs
are not crotchety. Plants with a long history and a wide
distribution at the hands of man are not of an exacting
nature, and make the best of it, like seasoned travellers.

But there are plenty of books and pamphlets con-
cerned with the making of borders and beds, plenty of
leaflets about composts and manures and other hearty
matters, and I do not intend to go into this elementary
side of garden-making. Gardeners worth their salt, moreover, will all have their own pet beliefs, hopes, methods,
and materials. There is one hint worth passing on to
those who might occasionally prepare a border in the
grand manner, which is that a virtue resides in the

eighteenth-century practice of putting at the bottom of a well-dug trench a couch of branched saplings or open brush before the enriched earth is replaced. Where the lower soil is heavy and clinging, this antique usage makes for better drainage, and permits deep roots to find their way into the ground. With ordinary "good garden soil" a proper cleaning-up in the fall and a top dressing of old manure is sufficient, though it is also a good plan to rake in some hardwood ashes and a light couch of old dressing in the spring. Too rich a soil breeds watery stems, susceptibility to moulds and rankness of growth at the expense of flowers in many plants, though some will gorge and thrive on it, whilst others ungratefully sicken and stand still.

If the herbs are going to be arranged in a border, and the garden can manage it, it is well to have two beds, one with a direct southern exposure, one with an exposure due east or a little south of east. This is what I have here and find most successful. In dealing with plants from other countries, agriculture and gardening do not make enough of a study of the quality of the light or the nature of the effects of the American sun. Our sun is a fierce and barbaric force, an Aztec presence, and the relation to it of the sun of Europe is the relation of a drawing of Zeus by Flaxman to a mythological figure chiselled upon a pillar at Copan. Many European plants, even those from the south of Europe and the Mediterranean, often have a quelled look in American borders, especially those planted against a western or southwestern wall. The blaze is too much for the shorn lamb, and what such plants need is not so much "shade" as fewer hours of our intenser light. It is for this reason that I like borders with various exposures; they enable one to give plants the amount of our sun they need and can use. Though I have various plants (not herbs) growing in the full weight of a summer afternoon (there are seasoned native plants and tropical upland plants well suited to it) I like the herbs to be in complete shade by the latter part of the afternoon, for by then they have had enough of sun. Under this regimen my herbs flourish. The Thymes get most sun, but I do not give Lavender the entire day of it, much to its profit. In a garden in the open, plants simply have to go through with it, which they do well enough.

Quite apart from the matter of the duration of direct light, certain plants prefer that the light they are given should be tempered, and these I have indicated by the use of the words "broken shade." In giving our plants "shade" we rely too much, I think, on the full blanketing shadows of walls or close-growing trees, and not enough on the shade developed within the border itself. A blanket of shade, like the sun turning the corner of a house in full force can come down on a plant like the wolf on the fold. Sometimes the solid shadow of a wall is inevitable and very necessary, but more often the broken and living shade of leaves in movement above them is a better kind of thing. I try to do this here, putting plants which are not genuine sun-haters in the shade and shelter of taller things. The practice is experimental and needs garden judgment, but the results are good.

To write at length about the watering of plants would again seem to me a folly, for any garden is the child of weather and a thousand circumstances, and only garden judgment can tell a gardener when and how much to use. To water late at night, indeed just before

putting the house to bed, is a counsel of perfection, but
it is the best thing one can do for a small garden during
a spell of great heat and drying-out of the soil. Seedlings
and cherished plants establishing themselves should be
watered with rain water from a rain barrel kept for that
purpose, warmish rain water being an *elixir vitae* to
plants. If gardeners will forget a little the phrase "watering the plants" and think of watering as a matter of
"watering the earth" under the plants, keeping up its
moisture content and gauging its need, the garden will
get on very well. It is all tentative; there are times when
a garden needs water every night and needs it badly,
there are times when an occasional deep soaking is all
that it requires. We do not mulch things enough in
America during the crest of our hot weather. Another
point to be remembered is that one is working with at
least two separate types of plants, a Mediterranean
group which needs water in moderate quantities and a
group of Mints which like a conventional dousing. Do
not, however, actually stint the Mediterranean plants
of their water, for in spite of their reputation they are
not natives of a "dry" region, and it has been my experience that they do not thrive in our Northeast in dry
and sunbaked situations. They do well in England in
a conventional border, and a like situation is the best
place for them here.

Shade-appreciating Mints, sun-loving Thymes, each
to its place, and may the garden thrive! The Mints need
not be plunged in Stygian shade. They like their share
of sun and thrive and blossom the better for it, particularly Peppermint and Applemint. The east border is the
place for them, with its fewer hours of direct sun; if
they have to stand in a south border, then it is well to

temper the light received. Entirely apart from the matter of light and shade, two of the mint species, Spearmint and Monk's Herb, should never be put in the actual border, for they are merciless spreaders and grasping colonizers. All other mints can be held in check, even Bee-Balm, whose newer hybrid forms are appallingly vigorous. If there is room for it, it is always well to have an extension garden of herbs in which one can root cuttings, put thriving divisions, and test new varieties and seeds. New plants of shade-appreciating things should have almost complete shade till they are established, and sun-loving things only a ration of the light which they can later sustain.

2

The annuals used in the border should always be selected and featured plants. Sow the seed carefully, being willing to have patience and take time, spacing the larger seeds by hand and avoiding a smother of the smaller kinds. When they come up and are safe to handle, choose the strong seedlings and put aside one and a half the number of plants you intend to use. If your seeds are in a flat, cover it with glass and wipe off the moisture once a day till the plants are seen, then leave off the cover. And get them into the border as soon as it seems safe, and protect them awhile from slugs and other devourers of leaves near the ground. Perennial seeds take longer to appear, and many are best started early in the house so that the plants may be adequately well grown before the frosts. Seeds and seedlings like warmish rain water, and transplanting is best done after sundown. If you wish to give some cherished plant every chance, move it at night—after having prepared the transfer by day. In making a transfer, I first dig a hole for the plant, put in a little rotten manure and loam at the bottom, pepper and salt the sides of the well with a little commercial fertilizer, flood the pit with water, go away and read a book, and then put in the herb with its ball of soil and fill it all in with dry earth, avoiding mud at all costs. The plant is then watered lightly an hour or two later. If herbs arrive potbound from a nursery, wash out the roots in a pail of water, keeping about one fourth of the soil in place, and then plant, opening up the roots as you put them in. Potbound plants have a kind of potbound complex and have to be forced out of it, else they come to nothing.

Because herbs are plants whose outer appeal is one of beauty and distinction of form, gardeners should try to have as good plants as they can and keep the whole garden ordered and thrifty. I always like to have the herbs, especially the taller ones, reasonably sheltered from the wind. When plants are thrashed about and bullied overmuch, the delicate feeding roots and hairs are apt to be broken or injured by the strain on the entire root system, and the plant as it stands above the ground acquires a blowzy look. Insect enemies are not difficult to deal with, having no special liking for herbs, and I have to do very little spraying. Only once in a great while will a pest visit an herb and have to be cleaned off, or a caterpillar solitary begin to riddle the leaves of Balm and Bergamot Mint. Monk's Herb is their favorite victim. Aphises are practically unknown, and if any herb of the selections should chance to attract them, take it out. The pests will come, however, if the gardener adds to the herb garden various associate garden plants which are not herbs, the Rose Geranium, for instance, in which the green aphis is completely and detestably at home. Slugs have a liking for absinthe, but of that I have spoken; in hunting for them at night, it is well to look around the edges of their canebrake, the Chives. And now a counsel to be spoken with the tongues of men and angels: if you have to spray anything in the herb garden, always spray with something nonpoisonous to human beings. Never, never, never use a poisonous spray anywhere near these plants of domestic and human use.

There should always be flower colour in a garden of herbs, but no conspicuously flowering herb or group of such herbs should ever be suffered to outplay the herbs themselves. This is an important point. Better too few flowering herbs than too many. I try to keep one border for herbs whose flowers are inconspicuous, letting the bed make its effect in subtleties and distinctions; the general "tussiemussie" beyond I open to both those with inconspicuous and more conspicuous blooms. None of the herbs I have listed will exactly overwhelm any border, but even then the distribution of flower colour is something to plan with care, a garden problem to which there are as many pleasant answers as there are gardeners. In planning the garden itself, I think it best to avoid awhile the making of just one more formal border of perennials. Herbs do not really lend themselves particularly well to backgrounds and masses; their variations of height invite more imagination and subtlety. Taller ones are often very lovely when treated as isolated pillars skillfully placed and closed in upon by shorter herbs of suitable heights, and once a gardener has come to know herbs well, there is opened a whole new world of garden

LAVENDER

making in which to note, enjoy, and arrange the beautiful and living harmonies of green. If the gardener will remember that herbs are living things to be used in living ways, the garden will come to living beauty by its own natural paths.

The matter of winter protection needs no special counsel. Many herbs are as hardy as plants of the north temperate zone can ever be, and those which need special winter protection have already been noted in the lists. The others the gardener can cover along with the rest of the garden in any favourite way he has found suited to his climate and latitude.

In gathering, preparing, and drying herbs, it is customary to cut the leaf stalks just before the plant flowers, the gathering to be made in the morning and on a warm sunshiny day and after the dew has left the leaves. All imperfect and withered leaves having been discarded, the herbs should be taken in loose, open bunches to some warm sunny room or attic and hung in the morning sun for half an hour, and then removed from the direct light and left to dry and crisp. When they have reached this state, the leaves should be stripped from the stalk, crumpled to the consistency the household prefers, and put away in sealed glass or china jars. Leaves for infusions or tisanes had best be left whole, and some prefer to leave them on the stalk and to keep a number of these bunches in a large, well-closed paper bag. Aromatic seeds are best dried by being shaken loosely upon a clean cloth laid in a wire box or colander standing in a warm place. In addition to tisanes and infusions and kitchen flavourings, all kinds of herbal patchoulis and potpourris can be made of the dried leaves and fruits. The skilled and imaginative have a field of their own in the invention of new and memorable cordials, the materials of the art being in their hands.

Not difficult to plan, not at all difficult to maintain, a garden of herbs gives more months of garden pleasure and more kinds of pleasure than any other. Its interest is independent of flowers, its fragrances are given from the first leaf to the last, its uses make it a part of the amenities of the whole year, and its history and traditions touch all nations and all times.

1. FRENCH NAMES OF THE HERBS CARRIED IN FRENCH CATALOGUES:

Agrimony, *Aigremoine*; Althea, *Guimauve*; Carduus Benedictus, *Chardon Bénit*; Fumitory, *Fumeterre*; Lovage, *Ache de Montagne*; Spike Vervain, *Verveine Officinale*; Woad or Isatis, *Pastel*.

2. TEN VERY HARDY HERB PERENNIALS:

Applemint (plain form), Lovage, Costmary, Hyssop, Balm, Angelica, Comfrey, Wormwood (A. *Absinthium*), "Valerian" (*C. Ruber*), Chives.

3. HERBS WITH SIGNIFICANT FLOWERS:

Borage, "Valerian" (*C. Ruber*), Cerinthe, Althea, Clary, Goat's Rue, Pulmonaria, Pot Marjoram, Woad, Pot Marigold, Lavender.

4. TALLER HERBS:

Angelica, Lovage, Bayberry, Perennial Fennel, Carduus, Bee-Balm.

5. HERBS SUITABLE FOR EDGINGS:

Camomile, Burnet, Parsley, Dwarf Basil, Dwarf Lavender (*L. Nana Compacta*).

6. HERBS WHICH WILL STAND A DEAL OF SHADE:

Balm, any of the Mints, Sweet Woodruff, "Sweet Cicely" (European and native forms), Comfrey, Angelica, both Pennyroyals, Pulmonaria, Woundwort.

7. HERBS RECOMMENDED FOR HOUSE PLANTS:

Purple Basil, and Summer Savoury (half a dozen seedling plants each to a flower pot eight inches in diameter): Rosemary, Lavender (*Lavandula Dentata*), Variegated Applemint, all three good as larger plants, especially Rosemary: seedlings or small cuttings of Rue, Germander, Caraway-Thyme, Wild Thyme, Santolina, Pot Marjoram, Bergamot Mint, Balm, and English Pennyroyal, all excellent for small pots: the Bergamot and the Balm tending to assume a rather sprawly habit, the E. Pennyroyal being a true ground-runner. Those interested should try their individual luck with any herb which takes their fancy.

8. HERBS TRADITIONALLY ASSOCIATED WITH CULINARY USES:

The Savouries, Garden Thyme, Sage, Basil, S. Marjoram, Tarragon.

9. MEDICINAL HERBS MOST IN HOUSEHOLD USE:

Wormwood (*A. Absinthium*), English and American Pennyroyal, Peppermint, Horehound, Catnip, Balm.

10. HERBS FOR TISANES:

Camomile Flowers, Spearmint, Peppermint, Monk's
Herb, Sweet Woodruff.

11. GREAT MAGICAL HERBS:

Rue, Spike Vervain, Dill.

12. FLAVOURING HERBS FOR GREEN SALADS:

Burnet, Chives, S. Marjoram, the Basils, Chervil, Dill
(umbel and leaves); others may be found by the adven-
turous.

13. DRIED HERBS FOR FRAGRANCE:

Lavender leaves and Lavender seed, Rosemary leaves,
Sweet Marjoram, Costmary, Bergamot Mint and Purple
Basil leaves, Sweet Woodruff; Rose leaves may be added
for colour.

14. BIBLICAL HERBS DISCUSSED IN THIS BOOK:

Mandrake (Gen. 30, 14), Coriander (Ex. 16, 31),
Wormwood (Rev. 8, 11), Mint (Luke 11, 42), Cumin
(Isaiah 28, 25 & 27), "Anise"—the actual plant in ques-
tion seems to have been Dill—(Matt. 23, 23), Hyssop
(*Origanum Maru*) (John 19, 29), Saffron (Song of
Songs 4, 14), Rue (Luke 11, 42).

V

EPILOGUE IN SPRING

The earth emerges from the snow, lifting to the reassurance of the longer day her fields that have been as iron northward to the pole, a new green lies in the dappled warmth upon the hill, and the winter-barren trees are great with spring. All day long, blown by a new and warmer wind, loose ice and sailing floes from the ice remaining on the lake have come tinkling like hollow glass into the shallows of the coves, there to drift glinting out of the light into the shadowy green of pines once more reflected on quiet water, there to strand and disappear. The waters under the earth and the waters upon it are everywhere unsealing, flowing from the new green of moss down the slope of ledges in the sun and gathering in clearest pools where the snow has melted in the woods. Crows pass between the spring sky and the dead grass touched with green, a new odour of water and open earth is in the wind, a door of the house stands open, and from a chimney-top a wreath of smoke falls off and mingles with the sky.

In the garden of the herbs, where the drifts stood so high, blown up the fenceless slope and against the house from the northeast, the brighter sun stands warm. Beneath their autumn covering of leaves and hemlock boughs remaining green, the mother roots stir in the earth, coming to life in that darkness where, as George

Herbert said, they "keep house alone." Intricacy of leaf
unborn, colour drawn upwards out of the earth, fragrance and potency and beauty are here in secret being,
soon to be manifest to the several senses, and at their
roots a gift of the gardener's peace which none shall
have who have not a deep peace with the earth, though
the road to her seem but a path. For beside that path lie
the seasons and the ritual of the year, the vast adven-
tures and journeyings of the sun, the towering of a
wave to its breaking, the faithful wheeling of the moon,
the sound of rain when there are no more leaves, and
the furrow lengthening under the tug of hooves on a
morning in spring. Sustained and moulded of its immeasurable forces, it is by this mystery we exist, and by
its poetic power in our lives that we attain the stature
of human beings, having the sun to our right hand and
the earth and the seas beneath us; without it becoming
like the ghosts in Homer, houseless, and thin and dead,
and crowding and whispering angrily for blood.

The quiet of winter is wearing through upon the land.
Human voices which seemed lost in the vast of snow
have again the open earth beneath them, and over the
unfrozen soil, across field and pasture and darker wood
comes the bold and distant cry of chanticleer. What
a fine sound it is, that triple and unearthly cry, heard
here in the garden through the pale quiet of the northern spring. All the animal defiance of circumstance and
fate, all the acceptance and challenge of the animal
blood come with it into our human world seeking an
echo there, before melting away into the light. Pressing
on with the sun the furrow shall follow north the sun
retreating, and the earth shall be sown again and shall

part, giving life to the seed and to the herbs of man's remembrance, the ancient leaves dear at once to plough-man and woman of the distaff, to priest and golden-circleted king.

INDEX